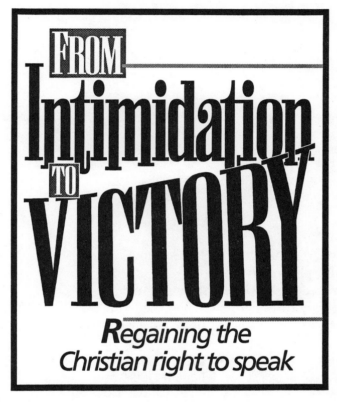

FROM Intimidation TO VICTORY

Regaining the Christian right to speak

JAY SEKULOW

Creation House
Lake Mary, Florida

Creation House
Strang Communications Company
600 Rinehart Road
Lake Mary, FL 32746
(407) 333-0600

DEDICATION

To my loving and loyal family, Pam, Jordan and Logan

ACKNOWLEDGMENTS ───────────────

I especially want to thank James Henderson Sr., Joel Thornton and Cynthia Turner, members of our C.A.S.E. staff, for their assistance in verifying the authorities cited and in preparation of various aspects of this book. I would be remiss not to mention the diligent work of Max Heine and the Creation House team for their invaluable assistance in putting this book together.

The thoughts contained in this book are not mine alone. I am deeply indebted to Harold Calvin Ray, Thomas Patrick Monaghan, Theodore Amshoff Jr. and William Haynes for their insight and partnership on our television program, "A Call to Action," seen on the Trinity Broadcasting Network.

Finally, I want to give my thanks to Jan and Paul Crouch and the Trinity Broadcasting Network family for allowing me to participate in their worldwide ministry.

"Now, Lord, consider their threats and enable your servants to speak your word with great boldness."

Acts 4:29, NIV

CONTENTS

ONE

RUDE, AGGRESSIVE AND OBNOXIOUS

THINK I KNOW WHY THEY call it the "high court." Start climbing those steps outside the United States Supreme Court and you feel as if you're hiking up to heaven. Pretty intimidating for a first-time visitor (and one with short legs, at that).

I ascended those steps for the first time in 1987. The brief time it took to move from the sidewalk to the inner sanctum of the nation's highest court paralleled the rapid unfolding of what was to become a cutting-edge ministry. It's a calling that would more than once bring me back to Washington, D.C., to defend religious freedom before the Supreme Court.

As I walked up the steps, I thought how God must have a sense of humor. A few years ago nobody—including me—would have suspected a Brooklyn-born Jew, then only thirty-one years old and a Christian, would be arguing before the

Supreme Court for the right of Christians to evangelize in public airports.

I arrived early and adjusted the podium for my five-foot, seven-inch frame. The last thing I needed was any handicaps, such as having to stand tiptoe to address the court. I knew that after six months of consuming preparation the skirmish would be intense but brief. Thirty minutes of back-and-forth with the justices, and winner take all.

Hanging in the balance was the opportunity to witness in the midst of millions of people. *Literally hundreds of millions.* The case had originated with the threatened arrest of a Jews for Jesus missionary at Los Angeles International Airport, where thirty-five million people pass through in one year. In Atlanta, Georgia, where I live, the airport handles forty-two million a year.

Many of these people are lonely, sitting around with time to spare, very open to the gospel. I knew the Bill of Rights, specifically the First Amendment, guaranteed the freedom to talk about Jesus with them. Who knows how many salvations, how many eternal destinies, would be affected by the decision of these nine justices?

Recognizing the Suffering Servant

So how did a Jewish kid from Brooklyn get involved with justices and Jesus? It certainly wasn't something I planned.

I was born in 1956 in Brooklyn but eventually moved to Long Island and lived there until my teen years. My family attended a Reform synagogue. I liked Friday night Sabbath services, though we attended only about once a month. Hebrew school was a different story. I think the only reason the cantor didn't expel my friend and me for misbehavior was that my friend's dad had donated the synagogue's plush drapes.

Religion was not a big topic of discussion in our home. Sometimes my father referred to the Supreme Being, but usually only at the holidays. I remember, when I was thirteen, trading insults over religion with a Catholic friend. We never got too serious about it, but I remember wondering if he was right. Could Jesus be the Messiah?

The thought left as quickly as it had come. I was secure in my Jewish identity, which excluded Jesus as redeemer. Though my family wasn't too religious, we reinforced our heritage by celebrating the Jewish holidays. My *bar mitzvah*, at age thirteen, was a glorious day: the end of Hebrew school and my passage into adulthood.

Two years later my family moved to Atlanta. My high school grades there ranked with my reading of the Torah at *bar mitzvah*—mediocre. It wasn't so much dullness or laziness on my part; it was just a lack of motivation.

As for hard work, I liked it. I was night manager for a large department store by the time I was seventeen. But as far as working on *grades*, well, that had to wait until college.

I planned to attend a two-year school for some business education courses, then go back to work. But a short stint at the local junior college whetted my appetite for learning. I decided to enroll in a four-year school. Little did I know the full spectrum of what I was to learn.

My desire to stay in Atlanta was probably the main reason I looked into Atlanta Baptist College (later known as Mercer University). The friendly, small-campus atmosphere was appealing. And it was only a five-minute drive from our home.

I asked my dad, "Will it bother you if I go to a school that calls itself a Baptist college?"

"Baptist-schmaptist," he said. "I'm glad you decided on a four-year college. Go ahead—get yourself a good education."

So I enrolled, determined to outsmart all the Christians. I did well in my pre-law studies. I attacked the mandatory Bible classes with a cynical confidence. I knew I could disprove the notion that Jesus was the Messiah.

What I hadn't counted on was Glenn Borders. Glenn wore a giant cross around his neck. I immediately labeled him a "Jesus freak." When we talked, though, I forgot about the big wooden cross—maybe because Glenn wasn't trying to shove it down my throat. He was active in college sports and student government and was a good student. He was there to help if you needed him. It was partly due to our friendship that my competitive attitude toward Bible courses changed to an attitude of genuine curiosity.

Glenn suggested I read Isaiah 53. The chapter scrambled my mind with its description of the "suffering servant" who sounded so much like Jesus. I must be misreading the text, I thought. Then it hit me—I had been reading from the King James Bible, a "Christian" translation. No wonder it fit so neatly. So I checked the Jewish text, but the description seemed just as clear. Still there had to be a logical explanation. No need to worry.

After I researched the rabbinic interpretations, I began to worry. Some of the earlier writings described the text as a messianic prophecy. OK, but who's the Messiah? Other Jewish scholars identified Isaiah or the nation of Israel as the suffering servant, but these contrivances were embarrassing. The details obviously described someone other than Isaiah or Israel.

I kept looking for another explanation, but nothing turned up. In the meantime, my Christian friends were suggesting that I read other passages, such as Daniel 9, which prophesies the Messiah's arrival. I went so far as to read the New Testament, which Jews are told is an extremely anti-Semitic "forbidden book." It didn't strike me as anti-Semitic. The apostles were saying the same thing about my people that Isaiah and everybody else had said: that we were stubborn and not very obedient.

As I kept reading, my suspicion was confirmed that Jesus really was the Messiah. But the decision was purely intellectual. I had wrestled with the question for about a year and was glad finally to put the matter to rest. I realized I needed a Messiah who would die as a sin-bearer, and I was grateful to have one. But for me to respond? That didn't occur to me.

A few days later I heard the Jews for Jesus singing group, The Liberated Wailing Wall. What a relief it was to see other Jews who believed that Jesus was the Messiah! Their music and message helped me realize that if I really believed in Jesus I needed to make a commitment to Him. They gave an altar call. I responded. It was February 1975. I was eighteen.

That night a lady I'd never met said, "If you get kicked out of your home tonight, you can stay with us." She caught me off guard. I had always had a good relationship with my parents—didn't smoke, drink or use dope. It hadn't entered my mind that my parents might be upset. After all, Jesus was a Jew. I was a Jew. What's the big deal if I wanted to believe Jesus was the Jewish Messiah?

The woman's remark scared me, and I decided not to tell my parents anything at first. But I woke up at 2:00 A.M., unable to sleep. I was close to my parents; I couldn't withhold such a major decision from them.

So I woke my father. I told him I had decided Jesus was our Messiah.

"You decided?" he said groggily. Of course, he was implying, Who are you to decide? He shook his head and said, "We'll talk about it in the morning."

15

Morning came, and he said nothing about it. Neither did I. Since I was living under their roof, I felt if they didn't want to discuss it, I should leave well enough alone. I had already been receiving Jews for Jesus literature at the house, so they knew this was more than a passing incident. We eventually discussed Jesus, yet they have never been hostile about my beliefs. They know I'm still Jewish. They know no cult has wrapped its tentacles around my brain and caused drastic personality changes.

Law School's Back Door

I finished undergraduate school with tremendous grades, but my law school admission test grade was low. Every time I took a review course I would score ten points less, so I decided not to take it anymore.

My first law school interview was with Mercer's law school dean. He said, "I don't care what they tell you after you go to the faculty interview—you be here the first day school starts."

The faculty interview ripped me to shreds. "You'll never make it here," they said.

The faculty encounter left me crushed, so the first day of law school found me at work at the department store. At 6:00 A.M. the law school dean called and screamed at me for fifteen minutes.

"I get one student a year just for whatever reason I want, and you were the one I picked. I told you to be here. Now get down here!" This time I took the hint. I went on to graduate second in my class.

I say all this not to boast but to show that God was preparing me for something. I had no idea what. But He doesn't give us five-year plans all the time. He often unfolds things bit by bit. If He chooses to jerk me out of a department store job and drop me in law school, that's His way. I can't argue. And God can surprise any one of us like that if we're completely open to serve Him.

I began my career in law as a tax prosecutor for the Internal Revenue Service. In one sense it was a miserable job; prosecuting people for fraud and tax evasion does not win you any popularity contests. But the trial experience can launch you into a terrific career if you win your cases—and I did.

I left the IRS to begin a law practice with a friend from law school. We had a monthly overhead of $1,600 and not one client. But with God's help we soon found business. We won some controversial cases and developed a good reputation. In less than eight months my firm was up to nine lawyers, two full-time certified public accountants and three paralegals.

While the law firm grew, I branched into a construction business. It occupied five floors of a downtown office building and was extremely successful.

Putting Up a Fight

As business flourished, so did my family. I had married Pam after my first year in law school, on my birthday, June 10, 1978. We had two sons, Jordan and Logan.

Meanwhile, I stayed in touch with Jews for Jesus. Though I began serving on their board of directors, I still was not giving vent to a desire that was growing in me: to use my legal skills to serve God.

Jews for Jesus had been distributing gospel tracts at the Los Angeles International Airport for fourteen years. For no apparent reason one day police threatened the arrest of one of their missionaries. I was asked to represent them.

"Look, get a lawyer in Los Angeles," I said. "The case

won't go too far, and every court in the United States has decided that airports are appropriate for evangelism. My goodness, they let in the Moonies and every other group that solicits money and does everything else. So why are they picking on an evangelist?''

I would come to know why two years later in Washington, D.C.

In the interim, people kept telling me they sensed that God wanted me involved in this case. No way, I said. Then suddenly our large construction business dried up—tax-code changes hit, and in three months it evaporated, with all three hundred employees out of work. We had lost everything, even our home. While we were financially bankrupt, God chose this time to reach down to me, and He kept me spiritually wealthy. For God to start using me, it took getting to the point where I could no longer control things.

I finally got the message. I spent the next six months preparing for a thirty-minute rendezvous with the Supreme Court.

When I was in Washington, I asked the Los Angeles city attorney why this case had gone all the way to the Supreme Court. He told me the reason—and this is an indictment of me and all American Christians—was that the airport commissioners *did not think Christians would put up a fight.* They had a regulation to test, so why not pick on the pious, placid Christians, who would do nothing more than fold their hands and fret?

Before the Supreme Court proceedings began, I looked back at the ''Christian row.'' There were my wife, Jews for Jesus representatives—and my parents. Whatever their feelings were about my beliefs, they were there to support me. And most important, God's presence was there. My wife, Pam, agreed that there was a supernatural peace and confidence in my presentation.

The city attorney went first. The justices sliced him alive with their questioning. It got so bad that—no kidding—I even prayed for the guy. It began to look good for us, yet I knew to expect no tea party when my turn came.

I was all set to launch into an eloquent Americana speech, our heritage of free speech and all that, but the questions started. The justices didn't stop firing for thirty minutes.

The court unanimously upheld the decisions of the lower courts that the airport's resolution to curtail First Amendment rights was unconstitutional. The passive Christians had fought back and won.

One of the big legal periodicals, *American Lawyer*, reviewed the case and judged my presentation "rude, aggressive and obnoxious." I decided this was accurate, or almost so. I don't think I was obnoxious—maybe rude, since I cut the chief justice off while he was speaking, but that was OK. Since he didn't give me a chance to do my opening, and there were only two minutes left, I was certainly going to deliver my closing.

Rude and aggressive? Yes. If you really believe what the Bible says—that Jesus is the only way, that outside our comfortable church buildings there is a world full of drifting souls, doomed to hell—then you have to be aggressive. Sometimes you have to be rude.

Actually, so often it's not the *messenger* who's rude and obnoxious, it's the *message*. Or, more precisely, it's the reception of the message. Those needing to hear the gospel are in the grip of Satan. If you enjoy darkness, even a little light is going to annoy you. Because so many people find the gospel annoying, those in powerful positions have no qualms about making evangelism illegal because it strikes them as rude and obnoxious. Consequently, it's become increasingly difficult for Christians to share that message with the freedom they have traditionally had.

That's why, after the Jews for Jesus case, I founded C.A.S.E.—Christian Advocates Serving Evangelism. The ministry is dedicated to defending the right to proclaim the gospel in public places. We deal with problems concerning access to parks, school campuses at every level, malls, street corners and, of course, airports.

C.A.S.E. was started because I saw a gap. There were already aggressive, effective Christian organizations that specialized in litigating religious freedom issues—the National Legal Foundation and the Rutherford Institute, for example— but I saw a growing need to challenge the state's infringement upon the right of Christians to proclaim the gospel. Robert Skolrood, executive director of the National Legal Foundation, encouraged me to fill that niche. With God's blessing, C.A.S.E. has been successful. Here are some of our victories:

• In New York City we won the right to proclaim the gospel at South Street Seaport, a large outdoor mall millions of people visit each year.

• We obtained an injunction against the city of Oakland, California, which had effectively banned handing out tracts near its coliseum. It took us a year and a half, but winning that case has helped open up other sports complexes throughout the country.

• The city of Atlanta passed an ordinance to prohibit the gospel from being shared on the streets during the Democratic National Convention. We obtained a temporary restraining order against the city and opened the streets for witnessing.

• In Chicago, the city denied a pastor the right to have a Christian carnival in a city park. A C.A.S.E. lawsuit got that decision overturned, and the city rewrote its regulation to meet constitutional requirements.

• In Tulsa, Oklahoma, a Christian ministry was sued for $40 million after it published a newspaper advertisement setting forth a woman's Christian testimony. We won the case.

• In South Padre Island, Texas, local authorities tried to prevent worship and evangelistic services on a beach where a half-million students would converge during spring break. Our legal intervention enabled the ministry to proceed.

I am grateful that C.A.S.E., in its brief existence, has been a part of these and other victories. They are truly God's, not mine.

At the same time, I do not mean to make it sound so simple. Most of these battles are protracted. Many are fought with scant personal and financial resources. They all involve spiritual warfare because the kingdom of darkness is clashing with the kingdom of light.

The good news is that while these cases represent only a fraction of the threats to religious freedom, the tide is turning. Where Christians stand up for their rights, the opposition is increasingly backing down. When courts are forced to examine the freedoms guaranteed in our divinely inspired code of law, more often than not the freedom to proclaim the gospel rises above Satan's smoke screens and lawyers' hot air. We are winning.

Nevertheless, there remains much work to be done. From coast to coast, religious freedom is under attack. It is not just a matter of dealing with a few anti-religious zealots in the halls of power. From the founding of this nation to the present, there has been a tremendous shift in our moral base. This change has been reflected in law—both in the bogus application of good law and in the passage of new, unconstitutional law. As you may suspect, the law is not being applied as fairly to Christians as it is to others. And by others I don't mean your next-door neighbors but pornographers, satanists,

New Agers and the like. Our loss of rights has been their gain.

As the Los Angeles city attorney candidly said, most people don't expect Christians to fight back. Will we? C.A.S.E. has already shown that some of us are willing to put on boxing gloves and step into the ring. But you don't have to have a date with the Supreme Court to stand up against abuse. You don't have to be a lawyer to know the law and demand that it be upheld. Every one of us can fight for our freedoms if we are willing to do so.

TWO

ENGLAND'S BOAT PEOPLE

MILLIONS OF PEOPLE every year stroll through the sidewalks and cobblestone roads of New York City's South Street Seaport. They browse in the shops, drop some cash, pick up a bite to eat and enjoy the colorful port scenery.

In 1988 they also had the opportunity to hear the gospel. That is, until security guards muscled in with their version of the law: no witnessing on the streets and sidewalks. So much for religious freedom.

Now drop back about 370 years, a little farther up the coast and the same issue: religious freedom. The Christians who were to land at Plymouth Rock were fed up with being muscled around in their native England. They took literally Jesus' command to sell all for the kingdom of God. Then they set sail.

One hundred and two people packed a space the size of a volleyball court in the Mayflower. They ate dried fish, dried pork, dried peas. With the hatches often closed because of stormy weather on the Atlantic, the stench, as the days crawled on past two months, grew that much more putrid.

But for almost half of the Mayflower's passengers—the Pilgrims—the physical restrictions of their trip were of minor consequence compared with the religious restrictions in their native England. There, a history of persecution arose from Catholicism and Anglicanism and mingled with the power of the state. The combination proved intolerable. So much so that they were willing to cram into this ship for a hazardous voyage to a relatively unknown place. It was a land where, farther south at the Jamestown settlement thirteen years earlier, some two-thirds of the settlers died of diseases soon after they landed.

Yet this experience did not deter the Pilgrims. They were like modern-day boat people who give up their possessions and risk their lives by crowding onto unsafe vessels to escape tyranny in their native land. The Pilgrims were willing to sell their belongings, agree to work for seven years to establish the colony and subject themselves to the uncertainties of a dangerous ocean crossing.

The Mayflower had no heating or plumbing. Halfway across the Atlantic, a main beam cracked. There were days when the ship simply drifted. Miraculously, the Pilgrims arrived safely, but sickness spread soon after their arrival. Half of them died in the first two or three months.

Nevertheless, when the Pilgrims emerged from the belly of the Mayflower in 1620, there was more than fresh air for their lungs and room to stretch their legs. There was freedom to believe. Freedom to worship. Freedom to pray as they wished. Freedom to govern themselves from a Christian foundation. Freedoms that, I regret to say, we can no longer presume to enjoy without interference, whether at South Street Seaport, in public schools or on our downtown street corners.

We can no longer take these freedoms for granted, but we can take them back. A woman sacrificed her job as newsroom secretary at the *Milwaukee Journal* in 1989 when she insisted on her freedom to picket abortion clinics. She was fired, officials maintained, because her pro-life activities damaged the paper's reputation for objective reporting. After she filed complaints of discrimination with the help of the Rutherford Institute, the *Journal* admitted its error in an out-of-court settlement. The flap also flushed out some other facts that no doubt interested the paper's Christian readers: Both the paper's parent company and the editor had made financial contributions to Planned Parenthood, the nation's leading provider of abortions.

All for Nothing?

In the Pilgrims' Mayflower Compact they wrote that they were covenanting in the presence of God to form a civil order to enable them to spread the gospel better. Subsequent developments in the founding of the United States of America further expanded the idea of a Christian nation. Guarantees of freedom to practice any Christian denomination as well as other religions formed basic building blocks for our nation.

These guarantees remained basically intact for two centuries after the Declaration of Independence. But by the Bicentennial in 1976 serious decay in religious freedom was underway. It has worsened since then.

In this book I will show you how enemies of Christianity

have routed prayer, the Bible and Christianity from every vestige of public education. At the same time, public schools are being used to indoctrinate children in evolution, New Age philosophy and sexual amorality. Even in private education the state jeopardizes the free operation of Christian schools and sometimes harasses those parents who choose to educate their children at home. The right to make a simple witness to Jesus Christ in public places—from street corners to the sidewalks of the Supreme Court—has been threatened. Acts of civil disobedience against abortion have been met with undue intolerance.

In a nutshell, *secularism now reigns in America*. It has replaced the Judeo-Christian ethic as the moral base for society. Secularists have successfully instilled in the public consciousness the idea that separation of church and state means suppression of religion at every turn. They have skillfully twisted to their own purposes the intent of our nation's founders—that there be no nationally decreed religion.

The result is that Christians have suffered a bad case of "rights rot." Dry rot is a fungal disease that causes wood to become brittle and crumble into powder. If your home's floor joists had this problem, it would be bad news. And the scary thing is, *it can happen even while the owner is completely unaware*. This is what has happened to Christians' rights of free speech and free exercise of religion. Because too many of us were apathetic and passive, we did not notice as rights rot spread throughout the culture.

The foundation has become unstable, but it is salvageable. Christians across America are doing their part to stop rights rot. Like the Pilgrims and the great figures of the Bible who faced seemingly great opposition, they are learning their rights and standing on them. They hear the call to action. They are responding fully armed. They can smell victory.

26

The call goes out not just to pastors, televangelists and Christian congressmen. It sounds to all who value the price paid by the Pilgrims, by the colonists, by the men who struggled to fashion a constitution that guarantees religious freedom while placing our governance under the sovereignty of a divine Creator.

Away With Tyranny

This call to action in its most extreme forms involves civil disobedience, which we will examine closely in a later chapter. Through my work with C.A.S.E. I've found that a little civil disobedience goes a long way. It's often required to test unconstitutional law and get the wheels grinding to establish the freedoms that others would take from us.

At South Street Seaport, for example, we were told that the area's developer, Rouse Corporation, had leased the sidewalk from the city. Rouse considered the public property as being private. So we indulged in some civil disobedience (based on Rouse's interpretation of the law) and repeatedly handed out tracts. I even went up there and distributed some to experience firsthand the harassment from the security guards and police. C.A.S.E. traded letters with Rouse. Sometimes the harassment let up, but it never completely stopped.

Well, the New York evangelists did not want to board a modern-day Mayflower and go looking for a New World to enjoy religious freedom. So we prepared to seek a temporary restraining order to allow the proclamation of the gospel. As I sifted through hundreds of pages of legal documents, I found a jewel. One paragraph said that, regardless of the sidewalk lease, *First Amendment activities must be allowed*. They could not legally suppress free speech. Reluctantly, South Street's lawyers agreed.

No one would have thought that a handful of evangelists would take on a major development company over what would seem to some like a minor privilege. No one would have thought that the band of Christians would stick with it for the long run. Certainly no one would have anticipated we would win, but we did. Sometimes God provides a Mayflower exit and a Canaan; sometimes He arranges a surprise third-round knockout, as we saw in New York. Frequently, I'm beginning to learn, He specializes in upsets.

Civil disobedience of a much greater magnitude than exercised at South Street Seaport played a major role in the forming of this nation.

The religious conviction of the colonists was that God, not man, had bestowed mankind with inalienable rights. When a tyrannical government interfered with those rights, it was time to throw off the shackles. While Christians acknowledged the scriptural injunctions to submit to legitimate government, a core group felt it was improper to tolerate tyranny, even from mother England. Finally they rebelled.

Up to that point, though, the need for religious protections had hardly lessened in the century and a half since the Pilgrims had landed. Quakers had been put to death in Massachusetts. Roger Williams, driven from Massachusetts because of his calls for increased religious and political liberty, founded Rhode Island as an enclave for the free practice of religion.

Consequently, when it came time to form a nation, the founders agreed that they needed an emphatic statement that government will not make a church. So when the Bill of Rights took effect in 1791, its First Amendment both prevented the establishment of a national religion and guaranteed freedom for expressing religion, as well as speech. Therefore, there was no problem with practices such as including chaplains in the House and Senate of the U.S.

Congress. James Madison and other presidents freely proclaimed national days of thanksgiving.

When the signers of the Declaration of Independence pledged their lives to the cause of freedom, they did so "with a firm reliance on the protection of divine Providence," a "Creator." Furthermore, with its assent to a spiritual authority above man, the document reflected the Judeo-Christian principle that man, as a fallen being, can never be completely trusted as ultimate lawmaker.

How true that is. I can tell you from the many city ordinances C.A.S.E. has dealt with that educated, respectable politicians routinely make decisions, and sometimes pass laws, that violate the Constitution. I don't think they're all motivated by a grudge against Christians, but their obstructions of our freedoms cannot be left unanswered.

It helps to know your rights. A group of small black churches around New York's Central Park had a rally in the park. Unexpectedly, with minimal organization or publicity, the rally drew twenty thousand people to sing hymns and to praise God. The report of police officers assigned to the event described it as one of the most orderly groups ever to march in the park, and that if they ever wanted a permit again, they should be given every favorable consideration.

The sponsors got better organized and planned for a bigger event. This time, even with the organizers' good track record, the city treated them as second-class citizens. They were asked to accept an alternate site. What do you do in a situation like this?

Just say no. And be prepared to appeal.

The National Legal Foundation, an organization that has worked closely with C.A.S.E., took the city to court. Once the city saw the handwriting on the wall—that the churches had a clear right to free speech and assembly in the park that in no way amounted to a government establishment of religion—the city relented.

Compromising for a different site would have cheated the churches and the many people who potentially could be touched by an outdoor service. Know your rights. If you're legally entitled to the whole enchilada, don't start giving away bites of it. God expects us to stay true to the full vision of ministry He grants each one of us. He wants to unleash victories for His people.

A Christian Nation

While the Declaration of Independence has references to a divine Creator, the U.S. Constitution does not. This indicates not a shrinking back from the value and function of religion but a growing awareness of the need to refrain from having a national religion—a need that was clearly stated later in the First Amendment.

On a more local basis there was already evidence of the integration of Christianity into principles of governance. Eleven of the thirteen colonies, at the time of the Constitutional Convention, had in their charters some provision that one had to profess Christian beliefs in order to hold public office. For example, a public officeholder in Delaware had to acknowledge that the Old and New Testaments were of divine inspiration. New Hampshire said the greatest stability for a state government was to teach moral virtues stemming from Christianity, and therefore its legislature was empowered to pay public teachers for that purpose.

This is not to say that the United States was a nation of Christians. But you can say that it was a Christian nation, founded on Christian principles. Though not all of the early leaders were Christian, there was a consensus that apart from Christian morality the whole grand experiment would flop.

George Washington in his farewell address of 1796 said, "Of all the dispositions and habits which lead to political prosperity, religion and morality are indispensable supports." James Madison, who is often cited as an opponent of church/state mixing, said that our government is based on the Ten Commandments. John Adams, the second president, was even more outspoken: "We have no government armed with power capable of contending with the human passions which are unbridled by morality....Our Constitution was made only for a moral and religious people. It is wholly inadequate to the government of any other."

A study through the University of Houston examined fifteen thousand writings by the founding fathers in the 1760-1805 period to see where their ideas originated. Three men were quoted most often: Montesquieu, John Locke and William Blackstone. Yet the Bible was quoted *sixteen times* more frequently than Locke and Blackstone. Scripture was quoted in 94 percent of the documents written by these men. Even the concept of three branches of government—the legislative, judiciary and executive—is rooted in the Bible: "For the Lord is our judge, the Lord is our lawgiver, the Lord is our king" (Is. 33:22). So how did we end up with the separation of church and state?

The Infamous Wall

Here's a civic quiz for you: Which one of these passages is drawn from the U.S. Constitution?

"Congress shall make no law respecting an establishment of religion, or prohibiting the free exercise thereof."

"In order to ensure to citizens freedom of conscience, the church is separated from the state, and the school from the church. Freedom of religious worship is recognized for all citizens."

When speakers pose this question to classes, churches or civic groups, only 40 to 60 percent of the respondents correctly link the first statement with the U.S. Constitution.

The second one comes from the Soviet constitution. So whose code are we following? The constitution of a nation founded on Christian principles or the constitution of a nation founded on atheism?

Supporting this apparent misunderstanding of America's most basic law on the church/state relationship was a 1987 poll by the Williamsburg Charter Society. It found that two-thirds of the American public believes the phrase "separation of church and state" is in the Constitution. Wrong again.

What is found on the same subject is the plain protection of the First Amendment in the Bill of Rights, limiting Congress but not necessarily the states. Its first portion covers religion: "Congress shall make no law respecting an establishment of religion, or prohibiting the free exercise thereof."

During our nation's founding, there arose considerable debate before the House and Senate arrived at that deceptively simple wording. It is followed by guarantees of freedom of speech, press and assembly. The first part—the establishment clause—covers the concerns about having a state religion. The second—the free exercise clause—ensures that no law, whether it deals with religion or anything else, will restrict the basic rights of Americans to exercise their religions.

So where did the idea of "separation of church and state" come in? Thomas Jefferson, as president, wrote a reply to a letter of congratulations from a group of Baptists in Danbury, Connecticut, in 1802. After quoting the First Amendment, he added, "thus building a wall of separation between church and state.''

I sometimes think so-called civil libertarians have quietly amended their copies of the First Amendment to add Jefferson's little phrase. They have magnified this idea to an unbreachable "wall of separation" between religion and government to justify every attack on the guaranteed free exercise of religion. Someone needs to remind them of the difference between personal correspondence and the Constitution.

If the founding fathers believed there was to be absolutely no relationship between the two spheres, how could the same Congress that passed this amendment in 1789 have called on the president to proclaim a national day of prayer? Or how would these lawmakers, on the same day that they approved the First Amendment, have passed a law declaring that religion and morality are vital to man's happiness and therefore should be taught in the schools? (This provision was included in the Northwest Ordinance, which established a form of government for areas not included in the states.)

And how about the man who privately penned the infamous "wall of separation between church and state" phrase? While he was president for two terms, Jefferson also presided over the school board of the District of Columbia. He installed the Bible as the school's primary reading text, saying it is the "cornerstone of liberty." In three treaties he negotiated with Indians, a provision of missionaries and a promise to build churches were included.

Earlier versions of the First Amendment's religion clauses reveal the intent of the framers: *that Congress should make no law that would establish one religious sect in preference to another.* Episcopalians in the South, for example, did not want the Puritanism of New England imposed on them.

Baptists were worried that Congregationalism was going to be established as the national religion. That's one reason they wrote Jefferson. Hence, Jefferson calmly referred to a "wall of separation" that would block the federal government from declaring a national religion.

Legacy of the "Wall"

In the second half of this century, as secularists have continued to spout their skewed interpretations of church/state separation, they have begun to reap what they sowed: separation. As Christians have stood by and watched this breach widen, "separation" has taken on a life of its own. Unfortunately, the separation is not the kind intended by the founding fathers. It is a separation of state from its Christian underpinnings.

In the place of Christianity, a newer religion, or faith, has taken root: secularism, or, as it is more commonly classified these days, secular humanism. As we will see in following chapters, there is no semblance of any wall separating *this* religion from its state.

Quite the contrary, secular humanism and a sometimes unwitting state have teamed up as an institutional Dynamic Duo. They fight against what secularists portray to be the oppressive, unenlightened forces of Christianity. They ignore the basic religious freedoms sought by the Pilgrims almost four hundred years ago. They deny the promise of religious freedom established by the U.S. Constitution two hundred years ago. Their brash challenge to the simple freedom to proclaim the gospel in public places, whether in the schools or on the streets, calls us to action.

The summons requires boldness. Before we can rebuild the walls of our spiritual and cultural heritage, we have to tear down the artificial wall that has risen out of nowhere to isolate anything resembling religion from the public square. I would not devote myself to this full-time ministry if I did not believe God was in the wall-building and giant-killing business. He has shown Himself faithful in the battles I've been engaged in. He is eager to do the same for you. All it takes is being bold in the things that are not seen—our faith—and bold in the things that are known—our rights by law. That's a Dynamic Duo that can't be beat.

THREE

MILITANT NEUTRALITY

S UPPOSE A YOUNG student asks his teacher, "Is the Declaration of Independence correct when it refers to the existence of God?"

A public school teacher in this situation is best advised to remain silent in order to abide by the spirit of many court decisions of recent decades. Any hint that there is in fact a God, a living deity, reflects theism, or belief in God. And public schools, so the logic goes, are supposed to be "neutral" when the subject turns to God.

But to communicate an inability to answer the question of God's existence is to promote atheism, or agnosticism—the belief that little or nothing can be known about God, if there even is a God. This is hardly a neutral thing to teach anyone.

Welcome to America in the latter twentieth century. Ours is a climate where Christian values are up against the wall, excluded from public education and used as a launching pad to further an anti-religious agenda whenever morality is in question. Freedom to share the gospel has suffered in the process, but the tables are turning. We must move out of intimidation and into proclamation.

Morality and Law

Many Americans still believe the cliche "You can't legislate morality." The adage is especially comforting for those who have certain habits they don't want to give up. It suggests the failure of Prohibition to stop the flow of alcohol or the inadequacy of laws against practices such as homosexuality or prostitution to affect what goes on behind closed doors.

Most Americans who subscribe to the impossibility of legislating morality have not thought through that idea. Any body of law is based on norms. It may be the Judeo-Christian norms, most simply expressed in the Ten Commandments. It may be broadcaster Ted Turner's ten commandments, a batch of environmentally conscious platitudes that he says replaces the "obsolete" decalogue given to Moses. Or it may be some other code. But in the final analysis any law expresses someone's morality. To prohibit murder is as much a moral judgment as to prohibit running a stop sign.

The idea of "You can't legislate morality" has itself become law. Courts—not to mention city councils, state legislatures and Congress—have been chipping away at religion and its morality for some three decades. All is done under the guise of a more pure separation of church and state. Religion is portrayed as the intruder, and the secular resolution becomes the neutral cure-all.

But this does not work so neatly. There is no void when it comes to morality. *Moral neutrality is a myth.* If you subtract the Christian perspective, something fills the gap. The teacher may not answer the student's inquiry about the God of the Declaration of Independence, but that silence points the student toward a specific view of the cosmos.

Those who attack religion under the banner of church-state separation dream of a pristine land where the law is completely "neutral." Such law would promote no one's religion or "morality."

"We don't want your abortion restrictions," say the secularists, "because you're trying to turn your religious views into law." Yet these same people see nothing religious about laws that prohibit murder.

"We despise your Bible that condemns homosexuality," they lament. "One sexual preference is no better than another." Yet they refuse to acknowledge the physical and emotional turmoil that surrounds the sordid gay life-style.

As we will see, these idols of neutrality are fantasy. Decisions must be made, and some moral framework, religious or not, guides the decisions. Before we examine what has quietly filled the role formerly held by Christian values, let's examine the foundations of America's legal philosophy. Let's see how proper it is that religion be rooted out at every turn in the name of neutrality.

The Common Law

John Wycliffe of England, a fourteenth-century hero of the faith known for the English translation of the Bible, believed that the Bible was of higher authority than the church. Therefore, all law should be based on the Bible. Growing out of this idea was a set of principles drawn from Scripture and applied by the courts that eventually became known as the common law.

In a sense, the common law has been around for most of

history. Because it is simply biblical principles—most notably the Ten Commandments—applied to law, it can be traced to Moses.

The common law worked its way into the English courts. Later it was incorporated into the United States Constitution and then into individual states as they adopted their own laws.

Though the common law became well integrated into early American law and society, its seniority did not guarantee tenure. Supreme Court Justice Oliver Wendell Holmes Jr., in his famous 1881 book *The Common Law*, undermined the role of common law. He theorized that the ''life'' of the law is experience—that is, it changes with the times—supported by the brute will of the majority.

Now you can study American history and find plenty of examples to illustrate Holmes's point. The problem is, when law goes with the flow, who knows where it will go? It acknowledges no absolutes. The Bible, full of absolute values and commands such as the Ten Commandments, has no place in formulating law under Holmes's philosophy unless the people happen to find it in vogue.

In retrospect, one might call Holmes a prophet. Relativism—such as situation ethics—has invaded law and society. The idea that, say, sex outside of marriage is absolutely wrong gets classified with dinosaurs. Instead, too many young people are learning that rightness and wrongness are relative to a situation. Militant neutrality dictates that anyone's absolutes are oppressive. They must be cast off. If religious freedom gets thrown out with the bathwater, too bad.

Militant Christianity dictates that God's absolutes reign. He did not run His laws through a church committee to see how they would affect attendance. He did not field-test them with a Gallup poll to see how they would affect His popularity rating. Holmes's legacy may be all around us today, but that doesn't mean we have to tolerate it. If we continue to assert the certitude of God's revealed law, the ever-changing law whose life is "experience" will fade to meaninglessness.

Banishing the Big Ten

The Ten Commandments would have created a lot less trouble for all of us in recent decades if they had come to us through Aristotle. But having come through Moses, a Bible figure, they have become embroiled in once-unthinkable courtroom controversy.

In light of America's debt to the common law, it goes without saying that the Ten Commandments are an integral part of our heritage. Even the avowed atheist, despising the very thought of God-given law, could acknowledge that the decalogue has a place, if only historical, in public schools. Some representatives of the American Civil Liberties Union— the organization most noted for attacking prayer in school— grant that religion has a *limited* place for study in the schools. Others, including certain judges, take a much more restrictive view.

In 1973 a court ruled in a Salt Lake City, Utah, case that a display of the Ten Commandments was legal because no one was forced to read it. No big deal—except for the idea that we needed a court to monitor the exposure of students to something as fundamental and wholesome as the Ten Commandments. But it didn't take long for things to worsen.

A Kentucky law mandated the Ten Commandments be posted on the wall of each public school classroom in the state. Private donations were to finance the posters. The law's purpose was to educate students about one of the basic moral pillars of the West's legal code.

Sorry, said the Supreme Court. In a 1980 opinion the court ruled that the law violated the establishment clause of the

First Amendment by promoting the advancement of religion. In language that is pathetically laughable in view of the plight of today's youth, the court said the commandments' posting could "induce the school children to read, meditate upon, perhaps to venerate and obey, the Commandments." Yet these same Ten Commandments are prominently displayed inside the courtroom of the Supreme Court.

The court's five to four split on this issue is perhaps indicative of an underlying misunderstanding about such First Amendment cases. Chief Justice William Rehnquist felt that because the commandments were part of our heritage, the primary effect of the Kentucky law was not to advance religion. In a dissenting opinion, he wrote, "The Establishment Clause does not require that the public sector be insulated from all things which may have a religious significance or origin."

Exactly. Many Supreme Court decisions—some of them majority opinions—have echoed Justice Rehnquist's sentiment on religious freedom cases. Justice William O. Douglas, speaking for the majority in a 1952 opinion, said, "We are a religious people whose institutions presuppose a Supreme Being." He also said, "The First Amendment...does not say that in every and all respects there shall be a separation of church and state." Courts have held that certain governmental actions that may tolerate or even aid religion, such as parochial schools, do not necessarily constitute an *establishment* of religion, as prohibited by the First Amendment. Rather, in many cases, the amendment's guarantee of free exercise of religion clearly outweighs petty worries about the seeds of a state religion.

But when the state bans the Ten Commandments from school and takes many other such actions to root out religion, does this create an absolutely neutral environment for learning? Of course not. If you pour out a glass full of water, you are not left with an empty glass; you have a glass full of air. By definition, when you remove religion from education, or from a legal system, you are not left with a void but with secularism. Like the air in the glass, it may not be so tangible—for example, you will not find many educators willing to proclaim themselves as devout secularists—but it is real and just as present. As we will see, secularism in its more popular form, secular humanism, has been identified as a religion. And with good cause.

Escalating Warfare

Look at the sex education in many public school systems. Adhering to this myth of moral neutrality, the most ambitious and liberal sex educators maintain that students need to be exposed to every facet of sexuality, including homosexuality and masturbation. Teaching that those things are wrong or that heterosexuality and abstinence before marriage are correct, they argue, would be to impose religious values in a system that is supposed to be "neutral." Rather, students should form their own values.

But the effect on students is far from neutral. The frank presentations of the details of male and female genitalia and intercourse, and the promotion of available birth control methods, including abortion, inflame the normal adolescent interest in sex. Furthermore, for students whose parents have instilled in them godly convictions about sex, a graphically "neutral" sex course can demolish those convictions. Chapter 7 will explore a case of Planned Parenthood's infiltration of the schools and subversion of parental authority.

There is nothing neutral about this process. It is, in fact, an assault upon our religious freedom. The opponents of traditional values, having driven competing value systems out of public schools, have wasted no time in substituting their own insidious system. When parents work for years to impart training in sexual morality to their children, and then the state permits teachers to undermine everything with another philosophy, it is no neutral cease-fire. It is war.

Fighting against our heritage, our freedoms to train our children and govern our society as Christians, is secular humanism with its Trojan horse of neutrality. God expects us to call the bluff on this charade. He has equipped us to do so.

First let's look at how it originated, how entrenched it already is and where it is going. Its adherents have only just begun to dismantle the freedoms of speech and religious exercise that our Constitution guarantees. The more we know how the enemy thinks, the more shrewdly we can attack.

FOUR

TODAY'S STATE RELIGION

A STORY IS TOLD about Johannes Kepler, the German astronomer and mathematician, and one of his associates who didn't believe in God.

The associate, noticing a beautiful globe in their laboratory, asked, "Where did this come from?"

"It's just there," replied Kepler.

"What do you mean?" said his associate. "It couldn't just be there. It came from somewhere, and I demand to know where it came from."

"Why won't you accept it when I tell you that it just materialized out of nothing?" asked Kepler. "After all, every day you're telling me that the whole globe we're on materialized out of nothing."

This tale illustrates a problem broader than what faces strict evolutionists who deny a prime Creator. It shows the bankruptcy of a worldview that begins and ends with man. This philosophy is best defined as secular humanism. I've seen firsthand how it underlies most of today's attacks on religious freedom in America. I've also seen it unraveling at the edges. I've felt the mushiness in its core—its inability to provide meaningful answers to any of life's problems. The soft underbelly of secular humanism awaits the fatal strokes of the sword of the Spirit—the Word of God—to finish it off.

What's So Bad About Humanism?

The term "secular humanism" was one of the most misunderstood concepts of the 1980s. Christians used it so freely that it became a source of media ridicule, a modern bugaboo that had no substance in reality. I wish it were that harmless, but it's not.

Humanism is a broad worldview that emphasizes the centrality of man. Both religious and secular versions have emerged in humanism's long history.

Humanism traces its roots to ancient Greece and Rome, but it is better known as a historical movement in Europe from the 1300s to the 1500s. During that period scholars rediscovered the classical writings of Greece and Rome and searched them for help in understanding life. Humanists were those who sought out these "humane" but pagan works, as opposed to the "sacred" writings.

The Greeks were the first to elucidate philosophies that we would call humanistic. In the fifth century B.C., for example, Protagoras wrote what has become a classic description of secular humanism: "Man is the measure of all things."

Partly in response to the church's overemphasis on the sinfulness of man, humanists began to exalt man and all his attributes. With its teaching on the wonder of man's potential and ultimately the innate goodness of man, humanism became the intellectual foundation for the cultural reawakening known as the Renaissance.

The initial curiosity in the ancient pagan writings grew to the point that some people began putting those writings on the same level as the Bible and then above it. By the 1700s theories of science and life began to reflect a view that acted as though God did not exist. All things were to be measured against man, whose pleasures and needs were foremost and who alone was able to satisfy them.

Humanism, then, in its secular form, believes society and law can be organized as if God did not exist. It holds that man can solve his problems by himself.

Secular humanism eliminates the Christian's God as well as all other spirit beings, but it does not—it cannot—eliminate the existence of an ultimate authority. For secular humanists, most commonly the buck stops with the state. In matters not ruled by the state—sexual morality, for example—the humanist's authority lies within himself.

Forgetting God

One of this century's most prominent examples of the state assuming supreme authority has been that of the Soviet Union. The state has severely restricted all forms of religion, though there has been some softening as the political climate in the Soviet empire has loosened in recent years. Historically, the corrupt communism practiced in the Soviet Union has vainly tried to make the state the provider of every man's needs in a "workers' paradise."

One of the products of this paradise, Alexander Solzhenitsyn, a renowned writer and former prisoner of the labor camps, recalled the Russian Revolution of his youth. He remembered people in his village asking, "Why is all this happening?" Others would respond, "Men have forgotten

God.'' Decades later, Solzhenitsyn said he could find no better explanation for the moral decay that affected not only his mother country but also the West.

Men did not forget God as soon as humanism flourished during the Renaissance. Christian values were very much alive. Biblical scenes still dominated much of the great art. Christianity was under attack, but it had not retreated.

What happened here was an overlap of two movements. The Renaissance most closely represented the emerging humanism. At the same time the Reformation was shaking the world of Christendom. As Christian authors John Whitehead in *The Second American Revolution* and Francis Schaeffer in *A Christian Manifesto* describe it, there was the "High Renaissance" in Southern Europe, making man the center of all things. Meanwhile, in Northern Europe, Luther and Calvin were proclaiming afresh that God is the center. The Renaissance implied a perfectible man in a perfectible world; the Reformation declared a fallen man in a fallen world, with no hope outside God.

These two worldviews are with us today. I have seen the artistic spirit of the Renaissance, with its emphasis on the wonder of man, at work here in Atlanta. When Christians tried to share the gospel with visitors to the Piedmont Arts Festival in a public park, they were stopped by police. I called the festival director; she told me she found the gospel message "distasteful." Furthermore, she said the evangelistic activities detracted from the beautiful artwork. When I spoke to her an hour later and told her of our plans to take legal action, she hummed a different tune. She agreed that, yes, we did have a constitutional right to be at the festival.

This may have been an easy victory, but it was no small one. In its ten-day run, the festival draws over two million people. Because a handful of Christians was willing to test the waters, share the gospel and call the bluff of someone in authority, the light of the original Creator shined in the midst of man's creations. It doesn't take a law degree to get the ball rolling. All it takes is knowing your rights and standing up for them.

As I say, the spirit of the Renaissance and the spirit of the Reformation are still with us today. They may not go under the tags of Renaissance and Reformation, but the principles are the same. I saw them clashing at Piedmont Park. Any system that exalts man, his creativity and his carnal reasoning above all else will find extremely distasteful a system that says man is a fallen creature dependent on God's forgiveness.

The Humanists' Creeds

You won't find many card-carrying secular humanists. By that I mean people who would readily identify with the American Humanist Association or subscribe to its virulently antireligious magazine, *The Humanist*. Nevertheless, there are those who are proud to affiliate with the organization. And some are well-known. The editorial board for the magazine, for instance, lists author Isaac Asimov, feminist Betty Friedan, Walter Mondale's brother Lester Mondale and behaviorist B.F. Skinner. The beliefs of these organized secular humanists have been clearly outlined in the Humanist Manifestos I and II.

Probably the most noticeable trait of their writing is atheism. An excerpt from the manifestos spells it out: "But we can discover no divine purpose or providence for the human species. While there is much that we do not know, humans are responsible for what we are or will become. No deity will save us; we must save ourselves."[1]

The whole purpose of life for the humanist is to build

49

heaven on earth. It has to be; the humanist neither believes in heaven beyond earth nor sees any purpose beyond the grave. Consequently, humanists define their own utopia and then set their own values—which are always subject to change—for the long road toward a better world. Anything for which there can be found a rational argument—abortion, sexual amorality or euthanasia—is adopted as long as it fits the jigsaw puzzle of the humanists' Garden of Eden.

Because humanists rely on themselves to save the world and progressively better the lot of humanity, they affect an intellectualism. In their own "distasteful" way, the humanists arrogantly regard Christianity as intellectually bankrupt. *The Humanist* writers spare no mercy when they talk about religion. They foam at the mouth when the subject of miracles comes up. To them, God, Satan and other supernatural beings are cartoon characters. Because secular humanists perceive Christian leaders as nothing more than charlatans, Christians are gullible buffoons who deserve to be bilked out of their money.

To a lesser extent, secular society as a whole enjoys thrusting this intellectual inferiority complex upon Christians. This is one mantle we must not accept. On the one hand, yapping dogs are more noise than anything else. Any group that is so shrill and unreasonable generally is defending a worthless point of view. So it is with secular humanism.

Furthermore, we don't put our hope in worldly knowledge or our ability to win a debate. After all, the Christian walk is one of faith—as is the humanist's, though of a different faith.

Nevertheless, there are times when we are called to action against this assault on the validity of our religious beliefs. For example, one of the humanists' favorite forums for denigrating Christian thought is the classroom debate over the freedom to teach creationism in addition to evolution. We must not retreat here. Christian scientists and other scholars have produced plenty of work to support a theory of origins that lines up with the biblical account of creation. Even some secular scientists have admitted that a prime mover is the best explanation for how the universe got started.

And how should we respond to humanists' claims that they hold the high ground of science when it comes to theories of origins? Kick out their shaky stilts. Their very foundation is obviously riddled.

For example, the humanist denies an eternal being, one who could have created the universe, and claims to accept only what reason and the senses can explain. But in rejecting a prime mover the humanist is left with this illogical premise: Everything came from nothing. Frankly, this requires much more faith than any version of creationism. So the humanists contradict themselves—denying the validity of faith while espousing a theory that requires enormous faith.

Undoubtedly, many learned people are among the ranks of humanists, just as there are equally well-educated, articulate spokesmen for Christianity. But what counts most is not knowledge but wisdom. As Paul wrote to the Christians at Corinth, whose culture already was steeped in centuries of humanism, "For the wisdom of this world is foolishness before God. For it is written, 'He is the one who catches the wise in their craftiness' " (1 Cor. 3:19).

During the 1984 presidential campaign, Christians began labeling candidate Walter Mondale a secular humanist, and with good reason. He had contributed articles to *The Humanist*. He participated in the Fifth Congress of the International Humanist and Ethical Union in 1970, where he said he considered himself a member of a humanist society "by inheritance." Furthermore, Mondale's views on abortion and the messianic role of the state paralleled that of secular humanism.

Once secular humanism came into the limelight it played in the press like the anticommunist McCarthyism of the 1950s. Secular humanism became the season's new dirty word. Unfortunately, this backfired to an extent on Christians, who were seen as silly paranoiacs trying to pin an unknown, all-purpose tag onto their enemies. That's OK. I'm grateful for all those who were willing to speak out, to write articles and letters to the editor. They helped shine the light on the slippery serpent of secular humanism that had been hiding for so long.

The media backlash over secular humanism's exposure was not enough to save Mondale. Voters thrashed him at the polls.

Secular humanism survived. It was tarnished a bit and for the most part slipped back into oblivion. For the enemies of religious freedom, this was just fine. Whether or not the humanists subscribed to all the beliefs of secular humanism, they did not want this new term on the table for discussion. They did not want to face the truth that they had been caught up in a philosophy bent upon limiting the freedoms traditionally enjoyed by American Christians. In their holy quest to root out every establishment of religion, they had committed the mortal sin: They had evolved into a religion, an established religion.

Religion Without God

Americans tend to think of religion as a Sunday morning affair of preacher, pulpit and pews, of belief in a supernatural God. However, religion can be any system of beliefs held to with ardor and faith.

The same is true of secular humanism. Christian author and activist Tim LaHaye notes that humanist writers refer to secular humanism as a "world faith," "a religion without a God," even "the next great religion of the world." Humanist Manifesto I says humanism is a "religious...point of view" and calls for the establishment of a "frank religion capable of furnishing adequate goals and personal satisfactions." In a 1961 Supreme Court majority opinion, Justice Hugo L. Black included "Secular Humanism" in noting that several of the nation's religions do not espouse a belief in the existence of God.

Secular humanism also has the missionary zeal of a religion. Humanists want to spread their doctrines. In another of their documents they have said:

> We have an obligation to expose and attack the world of religious miracles, magic, Bible worship, salvationism, heaven, hell and all mythical deities. We should be particularly specific and energetic in attacking such quack Millennialists as Billy Graham, and such embattled reactionaries as the Pope, because they represent the two greatest anti-humanist aggregates in our society.[2]

The implication is that everything beyond the world of appearances is an ignorant sham. Yet this sort of battle cry is the desperate rhetoric of closed-minded bigots afraid to confront the obvious—that there is more to life than meets the eye. There exists a spiritual component to human beings and therefore an entire spiritual realm into which they are plugged.

Because humanists deny God and the spirit side of man, they bat nary an eyelash when it comes to abortion. Man cannot be made in God's image since there is no God. There can be such a thing as lives not worth living because man, not God or His revealed law, determines who is worthy of

53

life and who is not. Birth control, population control or birth defects—these excuses and others more than justify legal abortion for the secular humanist.

In the humanists' world, sex has no necessary link to marriage or procreation; sexual pleasure is a paramount right, even for children. When recreational sex results in an unplanned conception, humanism says get rid of the inconvenient fetus.

Those who grow up believing that it's OK to dispose of unwanted children will have no problem seeing the logic behind getting rid of unwanted, burdensome elderly relatives. Euthanasia already is practiced in the Netherlands for terminally ill patients, and there have been moves in Oregon and Washington to legalize doctor-assisted euthanasia.

This is not to put words in the mouths of humanists; they support euthanasia and the right to suicide. The law has not quite caught up with them here. But if abortion is any indication, we can expect that it will unless Christians raise their voices and reverse the trend.

Again we see that the removal of Christian values from the public arena does not leave a harmless bed of neutrality. Secular humanism, whether it goes by that name or not, takes its place. As it does, noticeable things happen.

The next four chapters will show the effects of secular humanism's infiltration of public education. Our courts have supposedly tried to honor the First Amendment by preventing any establishment of religion in our schools. In the process they have turned around and violated the same amendment—as well as our most cherished freedom—by establishing secular humanism as the one tolerable religion.

The future of public education, as well as the opportunity for Christians to practice religious freedoms as they have for decades, depends on whether secular humanism remains the ruling philosophy in our public schools. As you will see, Christians are rising up to fight the intrusion of this pagan philosophy into our schools. They are fighting against secular humanism in its many appearances for the right to witness in schools, for Christianity to have merely a passive presence, in most cases.

The hostility against religion is sometimes unbelievable. But it is not unbeatable. The battles take many forms, and they are being won across America. I guarantee you there are opportunities to lock horns in your own school system. Whether secular humanism triumphs over Christianity in your community could well depend on the actions taken by you and your brethren in Christ.

FIVE

PURGING CHRISTIANITY FROM THE SCHOOLS

We thank You for the flowers so sweet,
We thank You for the food we eat,
We thank You for the birds that sing,
We thank You, God, for everything.

A CHICAGO KINDERGARTEN teacher used to lead her students in this innocuous prayer before they enjoyed their milk and cookies. But in 1967 the Sixth Circuit Court of Appeals put a stop to it, observing that some of the students even folded their hands and closed their eyes during the recitation.

In Albany, New York, Students for Voluntary Prayer sought official recognition from their high school so they could use an empty classroom to meet before school and pray. The principal refused. The students claimed the action

violated their constitutional rights and sued the school. Yet
the principal's decision was upheld in a federal district court
and the Second Circuit Court of Appeals.

The courts said permitting the meeting would have violated
the First Amendment's establishment clause, which prohibits
the state from establishing a religion. The court of appeals
was sufficiently alarmed to note that even a hint of school
approval for the students' meeting was "too dangerous to
permit."

I wish I could say these cases, documented in attorney Peter
J. Ferrara's book *Religion and the Constitution*, are isolated.
They are not. In fact, they are similar to the education-related
incidents in which C.A.S.E. has been involved. The Supreme
Court's 1962 ban on school prayer has snowballed to the point
that even moments of meditation for students are outlawed.
Until a recent Supreme Court ruling, the courts denied access
to students for after-hours prayer or Bible meetings across
the nation. Teachers have been harassed for having a Bible
on a desk or witnessing in a classroom.

If you think some of these examples are shocking, grab
an ice pack. You may need it to keep your blood from boil-
ing when you read about this persecution of Christian
students. Scott McDaniel, seventeen, handed a note to his
friend Matt Hinton in a hallway between classes at Henderson High School, near Atlanta, on November 21, 1989. The
note invited Matt to an off-campus meeting of the Fellowship
of Christian Athletes.

The assistant principal intercepted the note and suspended
Scott for three days. He threatened Matt with suspension.
Their transgression? *Possession of Christian materials.* Matt's
father, Bill Hinton, discussed the matter with the principal
and was told that if Matt or any students brought their Bibles
to school or wore religious T-shirts or buttons, they would

be suspended. Matt, in fact, already had been instructed once that day to put a jacket over a Christian T-shirt he wore to school.

Furthermore, these students were told that Fellowship of Christian Athletes could not meet on campus. FCA could not participate in any school activity, such as marching in the homecoming parade or having a group picture for the yearbook, unless the word "Christian" was deleted from their name.

Needless to say, the only relation "possession of Christian material" and the other offenses in this case have with the First Amendment is that they are vigorously *protected*, not *outlawed*. Of course, what is obvious in law, what is obvious to you and me, is not necessarily obvious to those in positions of authority.

The students and their parents refused to take this abuse. They began to make appeals. The good news is that C.A.S.E. has made some headway, and as this book is written I am hopeful the school will guarantee these students their constitutional rights. But it took a school board hearing and the threat of court proceedings to make this headway.

The bad news is: Why this hostility? this blatant discrimination? Why should anyone have to go to court to establish such simple expressions of speech and religion?

As we have seen, nothing in the language or original intent of the First Amendment's establishment clause—"Congress shall make no law respecting an establishment of religion"— requires that every vestige of religion be purged from the public schools. Furthermore, the free exercise clause— forbidding any law "prohibiting the free exercise" of religion—demands that all expressions of religion be allowed as long as they do not constitute the establishment of a state church.

Yet the penetration of secular humanism into our judicial and educational institutions has chased virtually every mention of Christianity out of many schools. At the same time, secular humanism, with its absence of moral standards and hostility toward traditional religion, has created a climate in the schools and the courts that has made the most offensive groups and practices welcome on high school campuses.

For example, in Rhode Island, self-professed homosexual student Aaron Fricke planned to take his male lover to the prom at Cumberland High School. The principal feared a disruption of the dance and refused to sell Aaron tickets. Aaron claimed a violation of his First Amendment rights to free speech and sued the school. A court agreed and ordered that he be admitted to the prom with his date. The couple's attendance would have "significant expressive content," the court noted.

Or consider an incident where the Chelsea, Massachusetts, school committee voted that a book containing vulgar language be removed from the Chelsea High School Library. A court agreed with a group of students and teachers who sued the school, arguing a violation of their First Amendment rights. The court ordered the committee to return the book to the library.

Again, these incidents cited by Ferrara are not isolated. When it comes to free expression of just about anything on the radical fringe, some school administrators and most courts have taken the broadest interpretation of the First Amendment. But when traditional religion is involved, a knee-jerk, heavy-handed application of the establishment clause has been the rule of thumb. Having examined numerous First Amendment cases, Ferrara noted other contradictions based on court rulings:

The Gideons cannot be allowed on campus to

distribute Bibles and students themselves cannot distribute Bibles or other religious literature. Yet nonstudents must be allowed on campus to distribute a "counterculture" newspaper containing profanity and students cannot be restricted from producing vulgar "underground" newspapers. Course materials teaching religious doctrines are impermissible but materials offensively contradicting the religion of parents cannot be questioned.

This kind of religion-bashing became national legal sport following the 1962 Supreme Court ruling outlawing prayer in school. Secular humanism was on a roll. The Christian community, for the most part, did not care enough to get in front of this swelling tidal wave. That began to change in the 1980s. C.A.S.E. and other Christian legal ministries and countless individuals are insisting on their freedoms in the classroom and on school grounds, and they're getting them. I can assure you there are more victories to be won before the turn of the century.

On God's Coattails

The erosion of the religious liberties of Christians is serious enough by itself. Yet as experts have looked at the expulsion of God from our classrooms, negative consequences have rushed in with startling immediacy.

The Supreme Court created a major turning point in 1962 when it struck down prayer in school. In his book *To Pray or Not to Pray*, author David Barton examined a wide spectrum of national data and trends to see if there could be any correlation with our nation's highest judicial branch giving God the boot.

He went to the U.S. Department of Education, the

Department of Commerce and other cabinet-level agencies. He traced forty-five key measurements from 1945 to the 1980s.

One of the indicators most closely related to education is scores on the Scholastic Aptitude Test (SAT), a college entrance exam. The scores were relatively stable up to 1962. Beginning in 1963, they began an eighteen-year tumble.

Barton found not only that SAT scores began a plunge in 1963, but also every one of forty-five social and economic indicators—such as productivity, alcohol consumption, sexually transmitted disease—took a turn for the worse in 1963.

This sort of theory, linking a spiritual cause with physical effects, tends to raise eyebrows, so Barton carried it further. He looked at other post-World War II landmarks, such as the Korean War, the Vietnam War, school desegregation and school busing, to see if any other factor could account for these trends. He found no one event that coincided with these post-1963 declines as clearly as the court's prayer decision.

As Christianity left the schools, so did its morals. In the 1940s the top public school offenses were talking in class, chewing gum, making noise, running in the hallways, getting out of turn in line, not throwing paper in the wastebasket and wearing improper clothing. By the 1980s campus naughtiness had some new names: rape, robbery, arson, bombings, assault, burglary, murder and suicide were the chief school problems.

When *Teen* magazine asked its readers to rate the main problems among high school students, suicide, alcoholism and drug abuse were among the top concerns. Sexual activity was the main problem, which shows that not all is well with those who are in the midst of a climate that encourages sexual experimentation. One study shows that by age twenty, 60 percent of all unmarried females and 81 percent of all unmarried males have had sexual intercourse.

You'd think the church would stand out as an example in this area, but it hasn't done much better. By the age of eighteen, one study shows, two out of every three students in the church are sexually active, defined in this case as fondling breasts or genitals or having intercourse.

The teen suicide rate shows a trend that also supports Barton's theory. His figures show that suicide among students has increased 451 percent since 1962. Among all other age groups suicides have risen only about 3 percent.

Drug abuse, of course, has seen a similar increase. The youth culture popularized it in the late 1960s, but it has since permeated our schools, public and private, as low as elementary levels.

This is not to say that schools are entirely responsible for sexual amorality among teenagers. Nor are schools to blame for suicide, alcohol and drug abuse. These problems originate in the home, not the classroom.

Parents must examine themselves first before blaming the youth-oriented social plagues on the decline of religious liberty in the schools. If parents are not spending sufficient time with their children and regularly training them from the Bible, they should not expect schools or churches or the passage of time to work miracles with their children's character.

In 1960 parents were ranked the number one influence in molding young people's values. Teachers were second. Today the leading influence is peers. Most parents will tell you that their children's peers are about the last group they would choose for imparting values. For example, three out of four students in one survey said they would go as far with sexual activity as necessary in order to escape rejection by their peers.

Of course, there are wide differences in the stability of family life that students have, causing a similar spread in students' resistance to peer pressure. But whatever the home environment, a central question is: Will the schools, without indoctrinating, simply *support* moral/religious training in the home? Since 1962 too much of what has happened in the schools has done just the opposite. By undermining prayer and all forms of religion, which could reinforce the training of many parents, the schools are missing an opportunity to reduce problems such as sexual laxity, suicide, and drug and alcohol abuse.

Going for the Jugular

The judicial system was only warming up in its sabotage of parental training and its attack on religious freedom when it issued the 1962 prayer decision.

• A 1965 case brought a ruling that it was unconstitutional for a student to pray out loud when he was getting ready to have his lunch.

• Also in 1965, the U.S. Supreme Court held that reading the Bible before the start of a school day was unconstitutional.

• In a Colorado case a teacher was told he could not leave his Bible, which he would read during his free time, sitting on his desk.

• The last chapter showed how a public school display of the Ten Commandments—by anyone's definition a foundation stone for the moral and legal codes of Western civilization—was ruled illegal in 1980.

• An Alabama law allowing students to have a moment of silence was ruled unconstitutional during the 1980s because it provided an opportunity for the teacher to suggest they use the time for prayer. Meditation, yes; prayer, no.

• In 1987 the U.S. Supreme Court ruled that public schools

could not require teachers to teach the biblical account of creation along with evolution.

And since the ban on classroom prayer, in many instances students have been blocked from using school facilities for religious meetings before or after school. This right has come to be known as "equal access," which means religious groups have the same right to use school facilities as the Spanish club, the computer club or any other extracurricular group.

A Supreme Court decision in 1981 affirmed that Christian groups on college campuses have the right to equal access. Congress solidified this right for high schools when it passed the 1984 Equal Access Act. However, until 1990, the Supreme Court never ruled on a high school equal access case.

This case began with a group of Christian students in Omaha, Nebraska. In 1984 they learned what Christians have experienced too often across this land—that just because you have legal rights doesn't mean someone in authority won't try to snatch them away.

Bridget Mergens, seventeen, and some friends wanted to start a Bible study club to meet on the campus of Omaha's Westside High School once a week for an hour. She wanted only the same privilege that was accorded other campus clubs; she did not even request school endorsement of the club.

The principal said no—separation of church and state would not permit it. The assistant school superintendent said no. Bridget appeared before the school board. Incredibly, they too said no.

Then a district court judge in Omaha seized upon a part of the Equal Access Act in a ludicrous attempt to justify the school's rejection of the Bible club. The act requires giving religious clubs equal access to facilities if the school allows other ''noncurriculum-related student groups'' to meet on campus. The judge considered that the club was not related to the curriculum and therefore did not merit the same access as the other clubs, which supposedly were curriculum-related.

In actuality perhaps thirty of the thirty-five clubs at Westside—the chess club and scuba club, for instance—were not related to the curriculum. Even school officials admitted that some clubs, such as the Welcome to Westside Club and Peer Advocates (for assistance to the handicapped), were not linked to the curriculum. To stretch the point even further, Bible study does indeed relate to a high school curriculum. It offers something to students interested in history, ethics, politics, literature and, needless to say, religious studies. Of course, this begs the real issue: narrow-minded hostility toward religion.

Recapturing Lost Ground

Incidents such as this show that the attack on religion in our public schools goes beyond prayer in school. The decisions of the courts and certain school administrators have trampled the basic First Amendment rights of free speech, free assembly and the free exercise of religion.

Recent signs have indicated that the tide may be turning. For the first time since 1962, the United States Supreme Court issued a positive opinion in a case involving Christianity in the public high schools.

On June 4, 1990, the Supreme Court changed its direction and handed down a decision stating that Bible clubs and prayer groups must be allowed to meet on high school campuses in the same facilities in which other noncurriculum-related clubs are allowed to meet. The court further held that the Bible clubs must be treated in the same way as other clubs.

This included use of the public address system, the school bulletin boards and the school newspaper and participation in the club fairs. In other words, the Bible clubs must be allowed to function as any other campus club.

This case is a great victory for Christian rights in America. Justice Sandra Day O'Connor, writing for the court, reinforced the right of "student evangelists" on campus. First Amendment rights of Christian students have been returned—rights they have historically enjoyed.

The antireligious momentum has gone so far as to produce censorship in the schools. Textbooks edited to pass through the secular humanist filters have so thoroughly screened out religion that the normal freedom of speech of authors has been curtailed, much to the loss of students. For example, you can find history books describing the Pilgrims as people who came searching for freedom, but giving no mention of their Christianity.

The next chapter will delve into the pitiful state of academic censorship, both in the textbooks of lower education and, incredibly, in the halls of higher education.

The sum of these assaults on religion is to restrict severely Christian students and teachers from exercising a basic tenet of our faith: to be the salt and light of the earth. No one is asking for the United States or any one state to establish Christianity as a state religion. We do need, however, to demand that every individual have the freedom to express his faith without government hindrance. Following are ways we can answer this call to action to bring the Bible, prayer and evangelism back into the schools.

First, *work toward a constitutional amendment to return voluntary student prayer and religious principles to school.* This means petitioning our senators and representatives to sponsor such legislation.

Such a bill should stipulate that participation in prayer or any religious activity be voluntary. There must be no official pressure on students either to participate or abstain from the activity.

The second plan for restoring religious freedoms to public schools is *taking existing equal access protections and running with them.* Christians at every college and every public high school need to test their right to assemble for religious purposes and challenge the administration when they are denied.

Third, *young people on every campus should be openly evangelizing.* We need to expose every school regulation, every city ordinance, every state law that conflicts with preeminent constitutional rights to free speech and free exercise of religion.

The Supreme Court has correctly stated that the high school campus is a marketplace for ideas. The gospel needs to be competing in that arena, not relegated to Sunday morning church services.

SIX

THE NEW CENSORS

MENTION "CENSORSHIP" and "school" in the same breath, and stereotypes come to mind for most Americans: a group of excited Christian teenagers burning rock albums and tapes, or some stuffy parents campaigning to remove *The Grapes of Wrath* or *Catcher in the Rye* from the local elementary school library.

The media enjoy focusing on these usually legitimate actions of concerned Christians. At the same time, they conveniently ignore more dangerous, deep-rooted censorships that are making a mockery of our educational system. This censorship is not limited merely to public education, where textbook publishers are giving us distorted versions of history and literature devoid of religion. Through the awesome power of the state, censorship is affecting even *private* institutions. This means religious liberties are being trampled. It's time to do something about it.

Libertarian Hypocrisy

Lawyer Clarence Darrow in the famous Scopes "Monkey Trial" of 1925 argued for the right to teach evolution in schools. He contended that to allow only one version of creation history to be taught would be intellectual bigotry. Fair enough. But what do we hear from the so-called civil liberties lobby and the U.S. Supreme Court today? That teaching both evolution and a science-backed scriptural account of creation is a violation of the infamous "separation of church and state."

Of course, we've already seen how "separation of church and state" is language found nowhere in the Constitution or Bill of Rights. Rather, it is the secularist interpretation of the First Amendment's protection of religious freedom while guarding against an official state religion.

The proponents of evolution are not content merely with equal access to the classroom. *They want to dominate that niche of academia.* If it sounds to you like the enemies of religious freedom want to have their cake and eat it too, you're right. Those who have traditionally fought for civil liberties in every arena—most certainly in education, the marketplace of ideas—have in recent years shown their true colors. Ideas with a link to the Bible simply do not fit their agenda. They would rather delete than compete.

The thrust of decisions by the Supreme Court and other courts has been to establish evolution as the Genesis 1 of secular humanism, the faith behind public education. At the same time, biblical versions of creationism have been booted out the door. For example, in the 1987 Supreme Court decision that struck down creationist teaching seven to two, one justice wrote that teaching creationism and evolution alongside

70

each other would be a "sham."

From Faith to Faith

Before looking at the educational travesty this narrow-minded approach has led to at the Institute for Creation Research in California, let's draw the basic similarities and differences between creationism and evolution.

Both evolution and creationism deal with origins—of man, of life on earth, of the earth and the universe. Both systems attempt to explain what we know about these areas and to reconcile often conflicting evidence, such as fossil records and geologic strata.

Evolutionists' standard argument for squelching "creation science" is that it is not a science but a religion. It's true that the historical records of Genesis play a major role in creationism. Yet the Christian scholars who have studied man's origins from a biblical perspective draw upon considerable scientific evidence to prove their analysis and to raise serious questions about evolution.

Furthermore, to emphasize the religious aspect of creationism is deceptive because evolution, too, is essentially a theory that demands faith. For example, there are unexplained gaps in fossil records and the basic evolutionary chain. And to go back to the very beginning of time, evolutionists cannot escape faith. Whether the "big bang" or any other theory of the universe's start is put forth, it necessitates faith: Since evolutionists reject a Creator, they must believe in the eternity of matter. It takes more faith to believe in eternal stars or gases than it takes to believe in an eternal Creator.

And as creationists have pointed out, the whole evolutionary system is at odds with the science that supposedly backs it. Entropy is considered a basic law of thermodynamics, the study of heat and work. Entropy states that things move from order to disorder. Heat dissipates. Energy decreases after performing its work. What is organized tends to become more random. It holds that the entropy of the universe is increasing because all matter tends to lose its available energy.

Entropy would tell us that life would, over time, become less ordered. Yet evolutionists maintain that the history of the world is one of increasing order regarding life, while entropy reigns in every other respect. Somehow, through a bolt of lightning or some other event, inorganic matter made a quantum leap to organic life. From this one-celled life evolved the entire spectrum of aquatic, land and airborne life, including man. Not only are evolutionists denying the law of entropy, but they are also making an exception to the principle of biogenesis: that all life must come from life.

A cursory study of any system of the human body—sight, reproduction, the mind—makes it that much harder to believe that such complexity and order arose from inorganic matter. It becomes ludicrous for the evolutionist to exempt his theory from the realm of faith. It is far more sensible to believe, as Scripture tells us, that man is a being truly formed in the image of a personal, living Creator.

In the Beginning Was the State

The Institute for Creation Research in Santee, California, had been operating a state-approved postgraduate program in creation science since 1981 when the program came up for state review in 1988. A state-appointed team visited to inspect the program. Three members of the team recommended reapproval. Two did not.

One of the objecting members wrote a scathing minority report. The state superintendent of education, Bill Honig, a known critic of creation science, reconvened the evaluation committee so it might reverse its decision. It did. The institute was notified that it had not passed reapproval because its curriculum included creation science.

The school appealed, and another team was sent. In early 1990, as this book was going to press, the second team was recommending denial of approval for ICR. Without state approval ICR, even though it is a private school, cannot operate.

This kind of intrusion represents several major threats to religious freedom. Most obviously, there is the state flexing its muscle against a private educational institution that accepted not one penny in public funds. If private schools are not free from state interference, then in effect *the state has a monopoly on education*. Intimidating religious schools is clearly a violation of the First Amendment's protection of free exercise of religion as well as free expression.

State monitoring of educational content generally follows the principle that state involvement should decrease as you go further up the spectrum. High school students are less impressionable than elementary students, and college students are more independent than high school students.

Certainly postgraduates—such as those attending ICR's program—understand the basics of religion and science and how they may overlap. If postgraduate students want to invest two or more years of their adult lives in a curriculum, they are obviously serious about it and know exactly what they're getting into. They don't need the state to meddle with the program because of some misconstrued notion about the role of religion in education, or because the state thinks it knows science better than the science professors.

What's happening to ICR is only the beginning of a crackdown on the freedom of religious colleges in California. Larry Vardiman, assistant dean at ICR, said a law that takes full effect on January 1, 1991, will no longer allow religious schools to be exempt from the state approval process. ICR already was non-exempt because it was considered a scientific institution instead of a religious one.

These kinds of trends represent tyranny of the worst sort. Not only is the state tyrannizing religion, but the state's educational elite are tyrannizing their own cherished free exchange of ideas. The American Association of University Professors' policy on academic freedom basically says you don't tamper with free inquiry. Yet many in the academic establishment have attempted to deny this same protection to matters that smack of religion.

This intrusion into the free exercise of religion is the sort of persecution that the Pilgrims and others sought to leave behind in Europe. America's founding fathers tried to codify religious protection in the Constitution, but here is yet another example of how, when Christians are not constantly guarding this liberty, their enemies are cleverly chipping away at it.

As bad as the ICR case is, it represents only a primordial phase in the evolutionists' vision for a progressive mankind to shed religion as if it were an outmoded limb. If California can cripple the ICR graduate program, then any state can attack any unpopular idea—Christian or otherwise, on the basis of any convenient state-written technicality—until the only ideas approved for education are those that fit the secularist agenda. *State approval then becomes a euphemism for censorship.* This is the same freedom of the concentration camp: You have the "freedom" to express an idea, but be prepared to suffer for doing so.

The education battles between church and state usually are not as complex as the ICR case, where two sides are arguing the mix of religion and science in a discipline where both elements play major roles. A state attack, as many private religious schools have learned, can be hinged on matters as simple as state-certification of teachers and as trivial as the ratio of bathroom stalls to students. Though parents may not see it this way, the public education visionaries know too well that religious schools pose a competitive and ideological threat. The more aggressive members of that establishment are not above utilizing the strong arm of the state to squash the competition.

Like the officials with ICR, we must be alert to the attacks on education at every level. We must be ready to dig in and fight legal maneuvers that may stretch over years. Such battles can be wearying, but they can be won.

Revisionist History

The more common form of censorship—tinkering with books—is well under way in the public schools. Judicial decisions restricting the free exercise of religion have resulted in a paranoid mentality among school administrators, some of whom would not otherwise be hostile to religion. It's a mindset similar to that of Deputy Barney Fife on "The Andy Griffith Show," who fretted that eight-year-old boys breaking street lamps were on the road to becoming hardened criminals.

"I say this calls for action and now!" he told Sheriff Andy Taylor. "Nip it in the bud!"

Nip religion in the bud or risk legal hassles. Just the mention of Jesus or the sight of a Bible causes knees to jerk from the teacher's desk all the way to the school board. And textbook publishers, eager to please bud-nipping school boards who want no part of lawsuits from the ACLU or People for the American Way, have committed embarrassing academic distortions to erase Christianity from even the most obvious places, such as history texts.

In other words, secularists have answered their own call to action. They have enlisted others in the education establishment in the process, often without the others' realizing it. Secularists have successfully put Christianity on the defensive in the most minor incidents, effectively trying to censor the Bible and other religious expression.

• In Manassas, Virginia, ten-year-old Audrey Pearson began taking her Bible to help pass the time on her hour-long bus ride to school. The principal forbade her to bring the Bible to school because of church/state separation. Audrey's family did not tolerate this distorted interpretation of the Constitution. By pressing the issue legally they secured Audrey's freedom to bring her Bible on the bus.

• A fourth-grade girl in Massachusetts put crosses in an art project. A teacher told the student she couldn't do that. The matter was challenged, and religious freedoms were explained to the teacher, who had not understood. She apologized.

• An Omaha, Nebraska, fifth-grader, after reading his Bible during a free reading period, was told he must take his Bible home. When the student's father asked the principal if the school library contained a Bible, he admitted it did. But, the principal said, that Bible was only for reference use and only by adults, and the law prohibits students from having a Bible in school.

This obsession with secular purity has surfaced in a more subtle way by gradually removing religious references from textbooks. For example, if you try to explain why the Pilgrims came to America without discussing the idea of religious freedom, as some texts have tried to do, you are playing fast and loose with history. Not only do you offend the Christian, but you cheat the entire class by presenting a heavily edited version of American history.

American blacks in recent decades have protested with valid reasons the minimizing of contributions blacks made to our culture. Since then textbooks have been written to reflect more properly the roles of prominent blacks.

Yet just the opposite has happened to the Christian dimension of men and women of American history.

Students at all levels are told of Christopher Columbus's motivation to seek a short route to the Indies, to seek gold, fame and glory. His religious side, if mentioned at all, is usually downplayed.

Columbus would qualify by today's secularized standards as a religious nut. He considered the meaning of his first name—"Christ-bearer"—a sign that God intended for him to bear the standard of Christ in a great way. He was fond of quoting Scripture in his journal, such as Isaiah 49:1,6: "Listen to Me, O islands [or coastlands], and pay attention, you peoples from afar. The Lord called Me from the womb; from the body of My mother He named Me....I will also make You a light of the nations so that My salvation may reach to the end of the earth."

More deeply than the motivation to search for a new trade route, Columbus was moved by a longtime sense that God intended him to bring Christianity to heathen lands. He wrote in his journal, "It was the Lord who put into my mind to sail from here to the Indies. The fact that the gospel must be preached to so many lands in so short a time—this is what convinces me."

It was no off-the-cuff decision when he named the first island sighted in the new world San Salvador, which means "Holy Savior." Peter Marshall and David Manuel document in their book *The Light and the Glory* how Columbus's men knelt on the newly discovered beach as he prayed: "O Lord, Almighty and everlasting God, by Thy holy Word Thou hast created the heaven, and the earth, and the sea; blessed and glorified be Thy name, and praised be Thy Majesty, which hath deigned to use us, Thy humble servants, that Thy holy Name may be proclaimed in this second part of the earth.''

Ignoring this side of Columbus cannot be shrugged off as a minor bias on the part of history writers. Rather, to withhold this information from students is censorship. I've heard of history majors who, when told this aspect of Columbus, said it was news to them. It's not that they slept through their high school classes. They simply never heard the full story. And these are the young teachers of today and tomorrow, all set to propagate a gutted version of history to another generation of unsuspecting students.

And Columbus is hardly the only victim of secularist attempts to revise history. Francis Scott Key was well-known for writing the lyrics of ''The Star-Spangled Banner,'' our national anthem. Rarely is it told that he was once interested in becoming a clergyman and that his poetry was religious.

Many observers hold that George Washington's many references to divine Providence and heaven were nothing but reflections of his day's popular deism. Yet his own writings reveal a profound Christian faith. Marshall and Manuel note that at the age of about twenty, Washington wrote a twenty-four-page book he called *Daily Sacrifice*, filled with beautiful prayers. In it he mentions God, Jesus, the Holy Spirit, forgiveness of sin, blood of the Lamb and being daily framed into the likeness of Christ. Other records later in his life show his continued dependence on God and how God intervened miraculously in the formation of our nation.

Paul Vitz made an exhaustive study of the wholesale censoring of Christianity from textbooks. He found that nearly 60 percent of the books did not even mention the religious roots of America in the context of studying American history.

Once publishers have spent years snipping religion from their textbook prose, the damage cannot be reversed overnight. But change can be wrought. Charles Haynes, author of *Religion in American History: What to Teach and How*, notes that the pendulum is drifting back. California—the same state that continues to harass the Institute for Creation Research—is leading in this change. A state education document "mandates much more inclusion of religion throughout the social science curriculum," Haynes said in a 1990 *Christianity Today* article. "That has pushed many textbook publishers to try to include more about religion, and we're beginning to see that happen."

Truth in Education

Christians face a major challenge to restoring freedoms in education. Secular humanism has seized the high ground in control of morality (or more precisely amorality) and religious content in education. To revise textbooks back to a semblance of fairness regarding religion will be a long process. Winning basic rights to express religion and to simply discuss religion in the public schools cannot be achieved quickly either, but it can be done.

The Caleb Campaign is a good example of what can be done. As part of its ministry to assert the rights of students and teachers to proclaim the gospel, the Caleb Campaign uses a monthly periodical, *Issues and Answers*. It contains news stories, interviews with sports figures and other items that help present a Christian perspective.

Students at a Colorado high school wanted to distribute *Issues and Answers*, but the administration balked. The administration even went so far as to pass a policy prohibiting the distribution of any material—religious, political or otherwise. The students appealed the policy without success.

79

Finally, students and their parents, recognizing that the school authorities had no right to censor their material, decided to distribute the publication. The students were suspended. Their parents, who were watching the distribution, were arrested. Parents and students then sued for violation of their civil rights. After two and a half years, the case was decided in their favor.[1]

In his ruling, the judge cited the same cases the parents had used in their appeals. This shows, unfortunately, how too many teachers, principals and school administrators need a lesson in basic civics. If we don't take the initiative to give it to them, no one will. First, of course, we have to know our rights before we can confidently proclaim them. Many Christians are like those of whom the prophet Hosea warned: "My people are destroyed for lack of knowledge" (Hos. 4:6). We must know not only who we are in Christ but what we can do as citizens.

Successes, such as the case in Colorado, are becoming more common. But they require people with the spirit of the biblical Caleb. He was one of the twelve spies sent out to check on the promised land. Only Caleb and Joshua were bold enough to give an encouraging report. Caleb understood something that most American Christians do not: that fear of man is rebellion against God. It is the opposite of faith.

The weakhearted spies saw the giants and feared. Caleb and Joshua saw the same giants and saw an opportunity for God to move. Christians facing an educational system that erases their heritage may perceive an insurmountable land of giants: principals, school boards, state superintendents, state textbook committees and textbook publishers. Let's view them with the eyes of Caleb and Joshua. Not one of them is impregnable.

We must fight to regain our basic rights to learn religion

in its proper context of history and other courses. We must resist illegal attempts at state approval or certification. To do anything less is to tolerate great infringements on our freedoms.

So great was the majority that overruled Caleb and Joshua that the Hebrews were doomed to wander forty years in the wilderness. May the church rise with a great voice and help all our brethren avoid a spiritual desert in the midst of this prosperous land.

SEVEN

REPROGRAMMING OUR CHILDREN

YOU PROBABLY WON'T find a First Secular Humanist Church, complete with pews and stained glass, in your hometown. Consequently, most people—even if they have heard of secular humanism—never perceive it as the nation's civil religion.

Yet, as we've seen, humanism functions in many ways like a religion. It has been called a religion by the nation's highest court and by its own spokespersons.

Nowhere is the faith of humanism, with its vain deification of man's potential and its bristling hostility to supernatural religion, proclaimed more openly than in *The Humanist* magazine. For those doubting Thomases who would feel more comfortable placing their hands on the steeples of the secular humanistic faith, John J. Dunphy pointed the way. Writing in a 1983 *Humanist* article, Dunphy identified his church in this declaration of spiritual warfare:

> I am convinced that the battle for humankind's future must be waged and won in the public school classroom by teachers who correctly perceive their role as the proselytizers of a new faith: a religion of humanity....These teachers must embody the same selfless dedication as the most rabid fundamentalist preachers, for they will be ministers of another sort, utilizing a classroom instead of a pulpit to convey humanist values in whatever subject they teach....The classroom must and will become an arena of conflict between the old and the new—the rotting corpse of Christianity, together with all its adjacent evils and misery, and the new faith of humanism, resplendent in its promise of a world in which the never-realized Christian ideal of "love thy neighbor" will finally be achieved.

Not all public school teachers, of course, are in lockstep with Dunphy. Some of them are not conscious of how ingrained the secularist bias is in public education. Many are devoted Christians.

Nevertheless, this militant war cry on Christianity in the battlefield of the classroom distills all the church/state conflicts that have erupted in the public schools since prayer was outlawed in 1962. And it clarifies phase two in the secularist attack on our freedom to study and proclaim the gospel: *After trashing Christians' freedoms of religion and speech, secularists are now aggressively replacing the Christian moral base with a humanist philosophy.*

Filling the Vacuum

Dutch philosopher Baruch Spinoza said that nature abhors

a vacuum. Certainly this is true with regard to ethics in public education. Excising Christianity from the schools does not simply leave a level playing field. The educational elite who dictate textbook content are not content to wipe the slate clean of traditional religion. They want to write a whole new philosophy onto that slate.

Unbeknown to most Christians, radical philosophies invaded public school curriculums in various communities across the country in the 1970s and early 1980s. Textbooks and exercises designed to inculcate feminist, socialist and secular values found their way into classrooms. The clear enemy was tradition. Parents and religion, as the chief perpetuators of tradition, were subjected to vicious ridicule and question.

This sort of intrusion often came under the buzzwords of "therapy," "values clarification," "behavior modification," "moral reasoning," "decision-making" and so on. By 1978 Congress finally acted on the complaints of parents whose children had been subjected to this state-sponsored brainwashing. Congress added the Protection of Pupil Rights Amendment, informally known as the Hatch Amendment, to the General Education Provisions Act. The amendment was designed to protect students by providing they not be required, without parental consent, to submit to any exercise that was designed to make them reveal information about their families and their personal problems, or their attitudes about sex, religion and other intimate matters.

Good law, bad execution. The Department of Education would not issue regulations to enforce the provisions. It would not even establish a procedure for citizens to file complaints, according to *Child Abuse in the Classroom*, a book by Phyllis Schlafly, head of the pro-family Eagle Forum. So after five more years of trigger-happy educators "clarifying"

85

traditional values into obscurity, after continuing complaints from parents angered at having their kids snookered into these experiments, the Department of Education held hearings around the nation in 1984.

Hundreds of parents answered the call to action. Many of them took on great inconvenience to travel to one of the seven locations around the nation. Their efforts were not in vain. Mrs. Schlafly's book compiles excerpts from the testimony given by parents at these hearings. Here are excerpts from just three of the parents who spoke:

• Archie Brooks testified about a Preventive Guidance and Counseling program used in Lincoln County, Oregon, during 1982. Parents discovered their children were being put through this class without parental permission. Questions asked of students in a classroom setting included: "Do you have a close relationship with either your mother or father?" "Do you believe in a God who answers prayers?" "Would you like to have different parents?" "Why did your parents get married?" "Do your parents ever lie to you?"

"In some cases," Brooks testified, "children were being alienated from their parents through expressions of moodiness, rebellion, self-centeredness and so forth."

• Dianna Storey told of an alcohol, tobacco and drug program called Here's Looking at You Two, which she said was in use in forty-four states. The course dealt with risk-taking. The teacher's manual suggested, Ms. Storey said, "that if students can take risks for the gain of high sensations, then risk-taking itself may be that substitute abuse." Some of the suggested risks were swimming nude with friends, lying to parents, having sexual intercourse and cheating on an exam.

While it might be argued that these are realistic temptations facing any high school student, the problem was worsened by the classroom approach on how to handle them.

Ms. Storey testified that "teachers are instructed that students are never to be told that any decisions are right or wrong."

• Jayne Schindler of Denver, Colorado, revealed a variety of horrendous experiences she had learned of in her state.

Traditional classes were pushed aside to make room for experimental ones: "Family living classes, sex ed classes, the bionomics classes to promote alternate life-styles so that our children would become more tolerant, abortion rights for minors, role-playing, lifeboat games and more Values Clarification."

She described a sex education book, *Show Me*, as virtually pornographic.

"Dirty words, disrespect for parents and authorities, are presented in many schoolbooks," she said.

In one class a newspaper article was read about a pregnant twelve-year-old. The class voted that abortion would be better in this case than adoption. An adopted girl in the class "was almost destroyed to have her friends feel that she was better off dead than adopted," Mrs. Schindler said.

A so-called English course for seventh-graders was called Death Education. Most of the stories used concerned death, dying, killing, murder, suicide and tombstone epitaphs. "One of the girls, a ninth grader, blew her brains out after having written a note on her front door that said what she wanted on her tombstone," Mrs. Schindler said.

"These courses openly admit that they are 'change agents,' " she said. "Change agents for what? Professionals for what?"

Circumventing Parents

Not content to drive prayer and the Bible out of school, the activist segment of public education sees a green light for their private agenda. They imagine themselves, as professionals, to know what's best for children. Many of the more than one hundred witnesses cited in Mrs. Schlafly's book tell of teachers belittling parental expertise and values and in some cases encouraging students to execute an end run on parental authority.

This is not an attitude privately held only by certain ambitious "guidance counselors." The National Education Association newsletter of December 3, 1984, warned its members how the Hatch Amendment could affect the way they could teach. Under the guise of "academic freedom," the NEA believes that schools do not need to be held accountable to parents.

The teachers and textbook authors who promote this new agenda would argue that they are not replacing Christianity with a new religion. Rather than "imposing" any sort of morality, the argument goes, they are merely assisting students to learn how to clarify their own values, to make their own decisions. In the process, though, they assume authority to demolish the traditional values of parents and religion. They incorrectly imagine that students can navigate life without a starting point of convictions.

What you have, then, is the old myth of neutrality. The phony neutrality that instructs a teacher never to pass judgment on students' evaluations of "risk-taking" is actually confirmed amorality—the belief that situations are beyond any firm judgment of being moral or immoral. This is one of the chief tenets of secular humanism.

Thanks to the outcry from concerned parents, the Department of Education finally issued a set of regulations to enforce the Hatch Amendment. Parents faced an intimidating giant in this case: the federal Department of Education teamed up with the NEA. It didn't matter. Years of foot-dragging by authorities didn't deter isolated parents around the nation who knew their rights and were not about to turn their children into laboratory rats for the mad scientists of education. Phyllis Schlafly's book notes that the regulations resulting from the hearings spell out what rights pupils have not to be subject to various tests and programs. The regulations also provide a procedure for filing complaints. (See appendix for details.)

Nevertheless, don't presume that your public schools are diligently avoiding all instruction that would violate these regulations. Those bent on reprogramming our children are still hard at work.

Homosexual Advocacy

Some of the high school students in the Los Angeles Unified School District were in for a surprise. Guest speaker Virginia Uribe told them that 10 percent of them were homosexual or lesbian.

Ms. Uribe, though, had a vested interest. She was a lesbian science teacher and counselor from Fairfax High School in Los Angeles. Through her tax-funded Project 10 she was out to recruit students into the ranks of the gay community, though she has denied this is her intention.

Students who were herded in to hear her speak at San Fernando High School recalled how she told them there was nothing wrong with the gay life-style, that it was, in fact, good. Part of her pitch was that gay students have more trouble than others with drug and alcohol abuse, suicide and dropping out of school. To help gay students, she offered referrals, such as to the Gay and Lesbian Student Services Center. At this center and others, students are plugged into rap groups where they can discuss their problems and meet other homosexuals and lesbians.

This is not simply a one-time, freak presentation. Project 10 is supported by the Los Angeles Unified School District, the Los Angeles City Council, the National Education Association, the California Teacher Association, the California Federation of Teachers and the ACLU.

The hypocrisy in this stings. Christians have had to go to the Supreme Court and Congress just to get permission for students to gather *voluntarily* on school grounds *after hours*, without official school endorsement, to pray or study the Bible. Yet here school officials assumed the authority to corral entire classes into a highly moralistic presentation that justified sodomy.

Sexual Indoctrination

Do not believe for a minute that these presentations even border on what normally passes for education. They indoctrinate.

First, they are based on lies. Project 10 uses the gross exaggeration that 10 percent of the students are gay. A more objective estimate, such as from the Centers for Disease Control, had roughly 4.5 percent of the 1980 population, including those with infrequent homosexual contact, as being homosexual. Other estimates are lower than that.

Another favorite lie of homosexuality proponents involves their Who's Who list of history's famous homosexuals that they use to justify this perversion. Granted, some homosexuals have achieved prominence. With many historical figures the evidence is hardly conclusive. But when it comes to citing religious figures—for example, all the popes and such Bible characters as David, Jonathan and Jesus—which some homosexuality proponents have done, they have stepped into the realm of fiction. It's also obvious they are out to discredit the source of their most authoritative opposition: Christianity.

A second proof that these advocates are indoctrinating rather than educating is that they do not tolerate normal academic inquiry. Students reported that Ms. Uribe would not entertain questions about the biblical stance regarding homosexuality.

Lest you be confused by some Christian denominations that acknowledge homosexuality as a legitimate life-style, know what Scripture says. Romans 1:26-28 describes how both men and women who lust for members of the same sex are burning with desire for that which is "unnatural." The outcome of this sin is that "just as they did not see fit to acknowledge God any longer, God gave them over to a depraved mind, to do those things which are not proper." (See also 1 Cor. 6:9; Lev. 18:22; 20:13.)

Furthermore, do not be deceived by the attempt of homosexual activists to portray their agenda as a civil rights issue. They would have the public equate their struggle with the struggle of blacks for equal rights, but such is not the case. There is nothing wrong with skin color, nor is there anything one can do about changing it. There is something wrong with homosexuality, and because its primary expression involves sexual activity, there is something one can do about it: abstain. The mental/emotional aspect for some homosexuals is quite difficult to change, but through Christian counseling and prayer it can often be accomplished.

Programs such as Project 10 may use the appearance of "counseling" to justify their intrusion into the schools. And they do, indeed, refer students to what they call counseling sessions. But a rap group where an adult tells confused teenagers that their leanings toward perversion are perfectly healthy is not counseling. It is conspiracy for moral and spiritual captivity. It assaults our freedom to utilize public schools without fear that our children will be immorally indoctrinated.

Project 10 starts from a radically different base from what

the Bible sets out: that there is nothing broken that needs fixing. The Bible tells us, and Christian counselors can confirm, that homosexuals and those leaning in that direction do need spiritual help and often professional, unbiased counseling.

Civil libertarians, as they purged Christianity from the schools, warned that Christians could take student audiences captive, subject them to moralizing and enroll them in a lifestyle that reflects that morality. Now a radical branch of those libertarians—avowed homosexuals—is getting away with the same scheme it screamed about. Our loss of freedom is their gain, multiplied many times.

Most school systems are not exposed to such an out-front recruitment for homosexuality. If your schools are, fight it. To admit such a program violates your rights to be protected from the state's establishing a religion—in this case amorality or secular humanism. There is no consensus that students need so-called "counseling" about homosexuality to discover some innate, perverse sexual identity.

"Everybody's Doing It"

Those who remain unaffected by the homosexual advocacy still have not fully escaped. They are caught by a much larger net—the libertine ethic that encourages sexual experimentation and, as a backup for birth control, abortion.

Parents of fourteen- and fifteen-year-olds in Missoula, Montana, were concerned. Their children came home with wild tales of a Planned Parenthood representative making an explicit presentation at school.

In a special documentary produced for James Dobson's "Focus on the Family" radio show in October 1989, students and their mothers described how the local Planned Parenthood director, Melanie Reynolds, brought to class a life-sized model of an erect penis complete with pubic hair and testicles. The model was used for demonstrating how to put on a condom.

One girl recalled that the Planned Parenthood presentation "made me feel like I was a nerd, or I was not cool because I decided not to have sex. They made it sound like everybody's doing it and you're going to do it soon enough."

Students also told how Ms. Reynolds promoted the availability of Planned Parenthood to help with birth control and that if pregnancy should result the organization could help with securing an abortion. Along with this aid was the benefit of confidentiality—parents need never know what's going on.

Ms. Reynolds denied using the model of the male genitals. Since the controversy over its alleged use, Planned Parenthood has switched to a model of a vagina, said Missoula mother Alana Myers in an interview separate from the "Focus" presentation. Mrs. Myers, a pastor's wife who has been a leader in opposition to Planned Parenthood in Missoula, said the model is presented—frequently by a man—who uses it to demonstrate applications of contraceptive foams and devices.

Freshman girls in the class told Mrs. Myers it "grossed them out" when the instructor put a wad of foam in his hand and ate some. He told them the foam didn't taste that bad, implying his approval of oral sex, she said.

Ms. Reynolds also denied the student charge that she suggested use of colored condoms for holiday "fun"—for example, red or green condoms around Christmas. However, she admitted the offer of colored condoms.

Whatever the exact nature of Ms. Reynolds's presentation, it does become difficult to give her much credibility when her organization is devoted to undermining parental authority.

Sandy McKasson, a former Dallas public school teacher who had attended a sex education training workshop, told how the sex ed teachers are schooled in communication skills:

> They are trained in overcoming barriers to sex education within the community. And Planned Parenthood knows exactly what they're doing. They are separating children from the parents by handing sex to them on a silver platter, and they know that their children are not going to come home and tell their parents what went on at the sex education class or down at the local Planned Parenthood today. The burden of proof is always on the parent in any community to try to prove that the sex educators are indeed seducing the children through various techniques in the classroom by opening them up to ideas, thoughts and feelings that they don't even know exist before the course starts. And then the parent has to come in and prove that this is happening because they're professionals, they're slick, and they deny these things.

George Grant, author of *Grand Illusions: The Legacy of Planned Parenthood*, told Focus on the Family that "Planned Parenthood openly admits that they are involved in revolutionary activity to incite social change." This includes sanctioning premarital sex and masturbation.

At this writing, Mrs. Myers and other concerned Christian parents in Missoula have not been able to keep Planned Parenthood from making their guest appearances at the school. But at least the battle lines have been drawn. The sex educators know they cannot get away with any liberal agenda that suits them without encountering vocal opposition.

Furthermore, Mrs. Myers said, it strengthens her

conviction to build a strong youth ministry that tells teens the truth about love, sex and abortion.

"Our main strategy is just continuing to try to reach the kids in other ways," she said. For example, a Teens for Life group holds rallies to protest abortion. "We're just trying to reach the kids with the truth and a positive message about their sexuality, and that is that it is a beautiful, special gift, but God intended it to be reserved for marriage."

Another Revolution

The U.S. Constitution, with its many freedoms, guarantees the right for groups such as Planned Parenthood and Project 10 to exist. I would not challenge that right. The right to exist, however, does not automatically guarantee these organizations a right to millions of dollars in public funding, especially when their goals contradict the goals of the majority of those who pay the taxes.

And most certainly these radical change agents do not automatically have the right to capitalize on public schools for the purpose of indoctrinating students in their warped ideologies. They do not have the right to violate the First Amendment by establishing a religion or morality—best defined as secular humanism—in state-supported schools.

Whatever rights humanists have exist only because parents have been too passive to notice what is going on and call a stop to it. In some communities alert parents have blown the whistle on improper sex education classes, sometimes even before they begin. That's the way to maintain control.

Grant is mostly right: Planned Parenthood is out to revolutionize American society. However, in another sense, the organization is only a step ahead of social reality that promotes sexual freedom. And not just sexual freedom for single people, but for married people, teenagers, children and people of the same sex.

In light of this, Christians are called to action for an even more radical revolution. We have been drafted to fight for the gospel. Always was revolutionary, always will be.

The manifestations of secular humanism, such as Project 10, Planned Parenthood and classroom therapy, need forceful opposition. But ultimately victory depends on the gospel—both the freedom to proclaim it and the effective outworking of it.

Homosexuals will not find the peace and normalcy they need because Project 10 gets thrown out of the schools. They will begin to find healing when Christians extend love and godly counsel. Likewise, teenagers, with their hormones raging, with movies and advertising encouraging sex, will not automatically refrain from sexual relations or abortions because some judge issues an injunction keeping Planned Parenthood out of public schools. They need an alternative. They need hope and a vision for a day when, in marriage, they can exercise their sexuality in fullness and meaning and freedom from guilt. Nothing but the gospel can offer a context for this.

Secular humanism has taken the high ground in public education, but the ramparts are crumbling. Christians with their moral antennae extended are picking up on the alien signals. They are blowing the whistle on immoral and sometimes illegal programs and meeting some success. If we continue to challenge humanist infiltrations of our schools, we can retake the moral high ground and re-establish traditional values.

ATTACK ON PARENTS' RIGHTS

STUDENTS AT THE Massachusetts school where Donald E. Kindstedt taught were asked to keep a journal. It was to be kept secret from their parents. As teachers would read the journals, they would sometimes say that religion was supposed to be kept separate from education.

In a 1986 interview with the *Rhode Island Pendulum*, Kindstedt explained how peer pressure and ridicule, combined with remarks from the teachers, eventually led the children to shy away from religious beliefs. At year's end, when he asked the students if they would like to sue their parents for giving them wrong information, most of the students raised their hands. It worried him.

"God is not a tyrant," Kindstedt said. "That was the view of God we were presenting when I was teaching humanism."

Kindstedt eventually bailed out of the public schools. He

and his wife, Alice, began to educate their three oldest children at home.

Though Kindstedt was through with the state's education system, the system was not through with him. When the Kindstedts submitted a home instruction plan to the local school committee, it was rejected because the Kindstedts refused to allow school representatives to visit their home to inspect the program.

The Kindstedts had answered the call to action this far, so they took it a step further and appealed. The couple wrote to the state that to submit to its standards "would violate our conviction that it is better to 'obey God than man.' " They said it would also violate their constitutional rights.

The education commissioner approved their plan. They would not have to let state officials inspect their program.

The Kindstedts won. Likewise, most of the home schooling parents who have to wrangle with local or state authorities over their programs eventually find a satisfactory resolution. However, when state officials from coast to coast take often combative postures toward conscientious Christians willing to make tremendous sacrifices to educate their children, it shows the true nature of the system.

These disputes raise basic issues of religious liberty. Who has ultimate authority over the education of a child? Since Scripture commands that we obey just civil governments, must private Christian education conform to the standards of the state?

How to Respond

Leaders of political and religious movements throughout history have realized a basic survival strategy: Control the training of the next generation and your ideology will live on. What began as radical can become commonplace in the space of one generation.

Consequently, those who would drive Christianity as well as all religions from the public square have focused most of their energies on the schools. The response from serious Christians—those who understand the depth of the secular humanism at work in the public school agenda—has taken two forms. One is fighting back in the public schools—both defensively, to preserve rights, and offensively, viewing schools as a mission field. The other form is withdrawing from what they see to be a corrupt and hostile system to private education, either in a Christian school or a home school.

We have already discussed the mandate for Christians to counterattack in the public schools. So let's look briefly at the public schools as an opportunity to spread the gospel, and then we'll examine those who've focused their energies on home schools.

To look on the bright side of all this, if the pendulum has swung so far from godliness in the public school system, then it represents a major mission field. The question is: Who should be the missionaries?

Children in pre-secondary classes, for example, are still forming their values and identities. High school students are as well, though many have developed firm convictions from which they can effectively let the gospel light shine. We have already seen examples of high school students not only pro-claiming the gospel but engaging the civil authorities in legal challenges to guarantee rights of free religious exercise for other students.

The Bible does give a few examples of young men—Daniel and his companions in Babylon, and Joseph in Egypt—who proved to be tremendous witnesses for God while being cap-tives of a completely pagan culture. While these are shining examples, they do not necessarily set the pattern for all young people. Scripture does not teach that sending all young children out as missionaries among their peers is a wise principle. Instead, there are admonitions in the other direction, such as Proverbs 13:20: "He who walks with wise men will be wise, but the companion of fools will suffer harm."

Ultimately, parents must evaluate their school options and the needs and strengths of their children. Then they can decide what is best for each child.

Teach Them Diligently

You don't need to fast and pray about whether God intended you to play a greater role than teachers in training your children. The Bible places sole authority and responsibility with the parents. Moses, for one, put it this way: "And these words, which I am commanding you today, shall be on your heart; and you shall teach them diligently to your sons and shall talk of them when you sit in your house and when you walk by the way and when you lie down and when you rise up" (Deut. 6:6-7).

From our twentieth-century perspective, it might be argued that the Deuteronomy 6 injunction applies to spiritual, not academic, teaching. Yet for the Old Testament Hebrews, there was little distinction. The training required for young people was intertwined around God's law. There was no problem with separation of church and state; it would have been virtually impossible even to define such a concept for them. The Hebrew code of law covered every aspect of life. As the book of Proverbs taught, the fear of the Lord was the beginning of wisdom. Everything sprang from a fear and knowledge of Yahweh.

The application of Old Testament law as a comprehensive religious/social code for God's people diminished after Jesus inaugurated the New Covenant. But the importance of the Bible as a foundation for all learning and training did not change.

Martin Luther understood this. He said, "I am much afraid that schools will prove the very gates of hell unless they very diligently labor in explaining the holy scriptures and engraving them in the hearts of youth." He went on to say, "I advise no one to place his child where the scriptures do not reign paramount. Every institution in which men are not unceasingly occupied with the word of God must be corrupt."

The Pilgrims also understood this. They were motivated by the desire to escape a corrupt system and gain the freedom to structure their lives in accordance with Scripture. They found the freedom they longed for in the New World.

In the nineteenth century, as public schools began to form and spread, they formed no threat to private schools. The public schools also did not threaten parents who educated their children at home, which was not considered the freaky practice that many people consider it today.

Tyranny in the Classroom

Humanist Charles Francis Potter made an interesting comparison of religious training and public schools: "Education is thus a most powerful ally of Humanism, and every American school is a school of Humanism. What can the theistic Sunday schools, meeting for an hour once a week and teaching only a fraction of the children, do to stem the tide of a five-day program of humanistic teaching?"

Answer: Not a whole lot. That's the reason why the biblical mandate for parents to train their children is more than simply a justification for home schools. More important, it speaks to a *responsibility*. The burden of children's spiritual training does not fall primarily on Sunday school teachers,

101

Christian school teachers or the church in general. The church exists to support those charged with training children in the way they should go: the parents.

About 90 percent of America's students attend public schools. No one else—not Sunday school, and usually not even parents—has the minds of these students captive six or seven hours a day, five days a week.

Worst of all, this vast training ground of the nation's public school system now has but one overriding philosophy—secular humanism. Americans are used to a free enterprise system guaranteeing diversity and low cost in virtually all goods and services. But when it comes to public education, what you see in one is what you get in all of them.

John Stuart Mill, a brilliant, home-educated nineteenth-century liberal, said education controlled by the government would be tyranny. When any entity has a monopoly on the schools, the result is indoctrination, not education. In the earlier decades of public schooling there was a remnant of Judeo-Christian values. Whenever morality surfaced in teaching, it generally reflected that common consensus of our heritage. Now the fallout from the church/state separation myth has virtually purged that perspective from the schools.

Freedom for an Alternative

In one case, six families were upset with what their children were asked to read in a public school. There were textbooks with the occult, mysticism and other things contrary to their Christian beliefs. The parents forbade their children to read them.

Both sides agreed that a conflict of beliefs existed. The question was whether the state could kick them out of school for refusing to read the material. A trial court said the system needed to provide alternative texts. But, on appeal, a circuit court said it was OK to give them the boot. The reasoning, in effect, was that parents who believe the way they did have no place in the public school system.

Courts are not the only ones reaching this conclusion. Many parents feel that the public school system, in conjunction with the legal system, is tightening a noose around their necks. They can stay in the schools only at their own peril.

For many parents the solution is a Christian school. Yet many parents cannot afford private school tuitions. Also, many energetic parents, especially Christians, want to assume full responsibility for the comprehensive training of their children.

The result is an exponential growth in Christian home schooling in the last few decades. A 1988 article in *Christianity Today* estimated the number of children in home schools between 250,000 and one million. About 85 percent of the home schoolers are evangelicals, and many of the others are religious, though not Christian.

Home schooling parents pay an enormous price to live out their convictions. While most could avail themselves of public schools, which their tax dollars are supporting, they choose to invest countless hours in personalized education. These are hours that could be spent earning money or pursuing other interests.

As if these parents do not have a hard enough time, the state has made life even tougher. Legal challenges to home schoolers across the country became so commonplace that the Home School Legal Defense Association was founded in the early 1980s and remains active. Most of the legal hassles have centered around teacher certification and testing.

Many Christians perceive home education to be a practice of the radical fringe and see no problem with state monitoring. The state does have a minimal interest in ensuring that children receive an education, but its intrusions into religious liberties in this area have far exceeded its legitimate concerns. These concerns fall into a better perspective when the effectiveness of home schools is separated from the myths.

First, *home schooling is not necessarily an oddball system of education*. Many famous scientists, writers and political leaders, including some of America's early presidents, have been educated at home. Public schooling, beginning in the last century in the United States, is a relative newcomer.

Second, *home schools produce quality*. Their students usually test well above the average scores of public school students.

Third, *home-schooled kids are not nerds*. The degree of isolation involved with a home school turns out to be an asset for socialization, not a hindrance. The students generally develop a stronger set of social skills and a stronger identity and are less likely to be influenced by peers. A parent would never expect his child to learn table manners by eating with his friends. Likewise, the student educated at home, exposed more to parents and less to peers, is more likely to be molded by adult examples.

Fourth, *professional teachers are not necessarily better equipped to deal with a child than are his parents*. Public school teachers are trained in crowd control. Studies of home schools show that parents, ranging from those equipped with doctorates to those with no more than a high school degree, produce children who test above the average for their ages. A teaching parent knows precisely the level of his or her own child and can tailor a program to meet the needs.

State vs. Family

This last point—teacher qualification—is where opponents have leveled their attacks. I'm happy to report a great deal of progress for the cause of parental rights and religious freedom. By the latter 1980s about seventeen states had no requirement at all for parents to qualify as teachers. The states feel the proof is in the pudding. If a kid tests well, mission accomplished.

On the other end of the spectrum, many states have required parents to be certified teachers in order to have a home school. Fortunately, most state legislatures have repealed such requirements.

In the early 1980s home schooling wasn't even clearly legal. Only three states had laws making it legitimate. By the late 1980s thirty-three states had gone on record to make it legal. Still, harassment continues. Superintendents have been known to ignore legal protections granted home schools. The practice of student testing has been occasionally conducted in a slipshod way that is tantamount to warrantless search and seizure within the home. As with so many other issues of school and religion, ignorance or misinterpretation of basic rights and freedoms guides the officials. The Home School Legal Defense Association has been involved in hundreds of court cases yet has lost only a few. And even those few were not complete losses—no family it represented has ever been stopped from having a home school.

Another area of conflict involves texts. Many states try to maintain their control over education by dictating what materials are used in home education. As with teacher certification and testing, the state becomes fixated on the *process* rather than the *product*. State control of textbooks gets back to the core issue: mind control. The state, or those state officials most intimately connected with public education, tend to want a monopoly on education. At least one court found a state's requirement of controlling textbooks to be unconstitutional.

Once they are attuned to the constitutional issues involved, courts usually are receptive to home school rights. State legislatures, though, are more susceptible to teacher associations. Home educators need to establish good rapport with their legislators and provide them with accurate, objective information about home education.

Those directly involved in defending home schools have seen a definite anti-Christian bias in some of the cases. Part of it is a knee-jerk reaction that Christians in court must be quacks or they wouldn't be there. Part of it is simply that when you tell a judge that you want to educate your children at home and avoid the "secular humanism" of the public schools, all the judge understands is that you are rejecting the fine schools of the upstanding community. Consequently, parents who find themselves in court over such issues cannot assume they will receive complete fairness.

When laws do not abridge your basic freedoms and parental authority, it's best to abide by Scripture and submit to civil authority. In 1984 Sharon and Ed Pangelinan of Decatur, Alabama, began a home school program to instill Christian values in their children. They did not file a necessary report to comply with a law regarding a home tutor. One thing led to another, and the couple was arrested. They moved to Tennessee and put their children in seclusion and were subsequently jailed for 132 days for refusing to bring their children before a court. All this produced great headlines, both in the secular and the Christian media, but the couple's apparent stubbornness to work with authorities' legitimate interests hardly advanced the cause of Christian home education.

Home educators must strive for excellence—both for its

own sake and to head off legal hassles. There are magazines that can help them in the pursuit of excellence and the freedom to operate without state intrusion. Workshops are available on how to keep records, how to choose a curriculum, how to handle certain subjects and how to administer discipline.

Compulsory school attendance laws (to put them in the best light) are intended to help ensure that children with negligent parents get at least a minimal education. Consequently, courts are most likely to uphold state intervention where the state appears to have a compelling interest in the welfare of a child. It's up to the parents not to give the state a legitimate reason to disrupt their home school.

Attention, Parents

Education, therefore, is a vast arena for God's call to action for parents. In the public schools, parents will determine whether Christianity is indeed a "rotting corpse," as committed secular humanists believe, or a light emerging from a bushel basket. Those who choose to have their children in public schools have two tremendous burdens: to train their children in the ways of the Lord and to know exactly what is being taught at school. This means getting involved—attending PTA and school board meetings, serving on textbook committees and personally monitoring certain classes. For the most part, these same cautions and responsibilities also apply to parents who put their children in private schools, Christian or otherwise.

The minority that chooses home education also has its work cut out in addition to the rigors of daily textbook learning. Regardless of legal protection for teaching children at home, there are always some public school activists eager to interfere with that basic freedom. Home-schooling parents will have to exercise constant vigilance to preserve their freedom.

The price of maintaining true academic freedom can be a high one for parents. It is a price worth paying, though, if it secures the training of the next generation. Education remains the cutting edge of the fight for religious freedom. It is a fight we can win.

NINE

FREE TO SPEAK, FREE TO CHOOSE

YOU WOULD THINK THE dissemination of information would find no more fertile climate than a college campus. And what better place than open-minded, laid-back California, the state that gave us the free speech movement from the Berkeley campus of the University of California.

But when it came to disseminating Christ, free speech was not free any longer.

From the pornography capital of the world—Los Angeles—came regulations that prohibited Jews for Jesus from freely distributing religious tracts on Pierce College's Woodland Hills campus. The school required the group to get a permit and then hand out materials from behind a table, where few people passed by. They refused. So police began arresting Jews for Jesus missionaries in November 1988 after they began giving out leaflets outside the school library.

Once it became clear that the organization was not going to submit to the college's regulation, the administration got tougher: They decided to seek a court order banning Jews for Jesus from campus. What sort of logic was motivating this assault on free speech?

The school's regulation was not meant to curtail free speech, explained James Norlund, administrative vice president at Pierce, in a *Los Angeles Times* story. Rather, it was to "maintain a certain level of order on the campus."

Or how about Judy Ponsor, an aide to the dean of students, in another *Times* story: "We don't want students stopped so they're late to class."

Forgetting the First

As these flaccid excuses hint, there was no good reason to keep the missionary group off campus. So why has it become necessary to argue for the right to free speech on a public campus? Isn't freedom of speech guaranteed in the First Amendment, which says Congress shall make no law "abridging the freedom of speech"?

Yes, free speech is guaranteed legally, *but there are entities routinely making laws to override that freedom.* Christians need to challenge these laws in every instance. Both the law and the Lord are on our side.

As we have shown, governmental officials and some courts have tended to lean toward the establishment clause of the First Amendment—forbidding legal action that establishes a state religion—in handling controversies involving religious free speech in public places. In doing so they have belittled the free exercise and free speech clauses of the First Amendment—our precious guarantee to be able to exercise religious speech and beliefs without government interference. This bias is beginning to change as Christians forcefully present their cases in court.

As the Pierce College incident shows, the right to free speech—the same right that allows the most vulgar pornography to be published and sold legally—sometimes gets unfairly denied when it is exercised by Christians. That doesn't mean Christians simply have to stop, moan and wait for the rapture.

While the Pierce administration was threatening to get a court order, C.A.S.E. went to work. As soon as we filed an application for a temporary restraining order, the college stopped the arrests, which by then numbered seventeen and had resulted in bedtimes behind bars for some folks. By the time we left court, the lawyers for the college conceded that the rules restricting evangelism were unconstitutional. They agreed to change the regulations for all nine campuses.

This opened a door to get the gospel in front of 120,000 students. Recently, the California Legislature amended Penal Code 626, which was used to arrest the missionaries. As amended, Code Section 626 specifically provides that First Amendment activities will be protected on all college campuses in California—this, of course, includes evangelism. As far as I'm concerned, if any one of those students receives Christ and is late for class, he got a bargain.

In some cases these roadblocks to freedom of speech and religion are thrown up by those—perhaps city council members—who are not fully informed of First Amendment rights and who want to stay on the "safe" side of the law. In other cases there appears to be deliberate anti-Christian bias on the part of those who would infringe on the elementary right to free speech.

In either event, what we have is a fundamental call to action. If Christians are not free to declare the gospel in open, public forums, they will be virtually limited to preaching to the church choir. A basic tenet of our faith is to let our light shine. Jesus explained (John 15) that the vine failing to bear fruit is good for nothing, fit only to be thrown into the fire. The Gospels show Jesus speaking almost four times in public for every one time He spoke in the temple. If He were here today, He would be in the shopping malls, the downtown sidewalks, the sports complexes, where the ordinary crowds are found.

The Bible calls us to follow that example, and our Constitution gives us the right to do so. Though laws and policies of recent years have made street evangelism more difficult, we at C.A.S.E. are seeing encouraging success in levels of arbitration as high as the U.S. Supreme Court.

A Conditional Welcome

Signs all over the place said, "The City of Atlanta welcomes you." As it turned out, some people were more welcome than others.

It was the summer of 1988. Atlanta put on its best face for the thousands of expected visitors. This leading city of the Southeast was no stranger to big conferences. But with the Democratic National Convention coming to town in July, there was more at stake than simply another major conference. This time national and worldwide media would be focused on the city.

While the media and the convention delegates were more than welcome, the Atlanta City Council had long before tried to make certain groups unwelcome: those who would practice First Amendment activities, including the distribution of religious tracts. A city ordinance prohibited evangelizing and other free speech activities in the area immediately surrounding the Georgia World Congress

Center, the downtown site of the Democratic National Convention.

The resolution of this dilemma took place in late March of that year, before the Democrats arrived. Atlanta missionary David Zauber called one morning and told me a police officer had threatened his arrest. David was handing out tracts outside the World Congress Center, where the American College of Cardiology was having an annual meeting. The officer gave him a copy of the city ordinance that prohibits literature distribution in that area.

One of C.A.S.E.'s basic operating principles is that we would rather *educate* than *litigate*. So I attempted for hours to negotiate with the city attorneys, but it was clear they would not budge unless there was a lawsuit. So we obliged.

By the next afternoon I was in court. The judge called us into his chambers. This was a little unusual, but he said he wanted us to review a "recent case," a Supreme Court ruling he felt would be controlling in this instance.

I was concerned. After all, C.A.S.E.'s ministry is dedicated to defending the right to proclaim the gospel in public places, so we stay up-to-date with all related court decisions. I prayed silently, "Lord, what recent Supreme Court case is this judge talking about that I don't know of?"

The judge pulled out a newly published opinion of *Board of Airport Commissioners v. Jews for Jesus.* This was the same airport evangelism case I had argued successfully before the Supreme Court and which had launched C.A.S.E.! If ever I felt the hand of God at work, it was in that situation. We argued the case, and the judge used the airport ruling as the precedent in issuing a temporary restraining order regarding the unlawful city ordinance.

In only thirty-two hours God had granted a sweeping victory. As a result, Impact '88, the evangelistic campaign planned for the Democratic Convention, was allowed to proceed. That week over thirteen thousand tracts were handed out. At least 150 people prayed to receive the Lord. There were hundreds of others who were prayed with, either to recommit their lives to the Lord or to petition God for needs.

Georgia governor Joe Frank Harris issued a proclamation of blessing and welcome for the efforts of Impact '88, proving that God had turned a bad situation into one for His glory. The governor even gave Impact '88 permission to hold a rally on the Capitol steps during the convention.

This shows how God is so eager to work powerfully in our midst, but so often He waits for people willing to take action. Had we not fought for the right to evangelize in public airports, and had David Zauber not been faithfully witnessing to the physicians, not only would those battles have been lost, but also the freedom to exercise the same right during that major opportunity in July probably would have been delayed until it was too late.

The Ultimate Freedom

The freedom to exercise religion is under siege. The freedom of speech is threatened. Yet the assault on freedom does not stop there. The ultimate freedom—the freedom to believe, or the freedom to act upon protected speech—also is not safe from outside infringement.

While angels in heaven are rejoicing when one soul accepts Christ as Lord, people on earth may be filing lawsuits about it. The freedom to share the gospel in public places is crucial, but in rare instances it can be negated if adults are not free to form their own beliefs and associate with others of similar belief.

Robin Polin, who was raised in a Jewish home, was eighteen when she accepted Jesus as her Savior. Ms. Polin, who is deaf, was brought to the Lord through the deaf education department of a church in Tulsa, Oklahoma. Because of her handicap and her age, her disapproving parents filed a petition for guardianship to try to remove her from the association of Christian friends. Another lawsuit was filed against the church for enticement of a minor and invasion of privacy.

The trial court, in a bad decision, initially found that Ms. Polin was mentally immature and appointed her sister as a guardian. Even if Ms. Polin was mentally immature, this does not amount to mental incompetence, which is required for the appointment of a guardian. Her guardian allowed her a limited amount of religious freedom but would not allow her to attend services with the preacher of her choice.

The community of the handicapped strongly supported Ms. Polin. Because her deafness was being used as an excuse to take away her rights, other handicapped people correctly perceived a threat to all their liberties from those who do not fully understand handicaps.

Even though she is deaf, Ms. Polin had demonstrated through sign language that she was fully competent. The Supreme Court of Oklahoma ruled that the trial court's action had a chilling effect on her freedom of religion and freedom of association. The court determined that she was capable of making her own decisions and gave her independence. She has since graduated from college. Had she accepted her lot with a guardian and practiced her Christianity in secret or with the restrictions imposed, Ms. Polin would not have gained the freedom she deserved.

Access to Other Turf

While some may be called to minister to a relatively small category of people, such as the deaf, many others feel an evangelistic call to spread the gospel to strangers. This means hitting the streets. And too often it means someone's going to hit back.

We've just seen how the city of Atlanta tried to block witnessing in the most public of places, downtown streets. Jews for Jesus had to go all the way to the Supreme Court to establish that Los Angeles International Airport, too, is legally open for free speech activities.

And I've discussed how a group of black churches had to threaten legal action against the city of New York when they were denied the right to hold a rally in Central Park. Such cases are not unusual. Municipal authorities will often try to direct a public religious assembly to another site. But sometimes this subverts the whole effort. Either the site may not be as nice or convenient or, if the thrust is witnessing and there would be smaller crowds present, the potential for evangelism is minimized.

Many times the resistance first surfaces when Christians inquire about a permit for a march or rally. There is no clear-cut rule that would apply to all cities as to when or where a parade or march permit is necessary. My recommendation is that you notify authorities if you will be having a public gathering in one place of more than twenty-five people. Personally, I don't think much of permits for street evangelism because city authorities do not ultimately have the authority to issue permits for such activity, though some may believe they do.

After all, you do not seek a policeman's permission to step on your car's accelerator when the light turns green. Likewise, you do not need some municipal bureaucrat to grant you rights that were declared two hundred years ago in the Constitution. Being too polite can leave you vulnerable.

On the other hand, if you're dealing with a major crowd don't just notify but seek help for crowd control, traffic flow and so on.

Taking It to the Streets

It would seem that streets are, without question, public forums. The Supreme Court has said so. Anyone who has witnessed the panhandlers of New York City can attest that free speech on the streets is alive and well. Yet when it comes to religious witnessing on the streets, situations like what happened in Atlanta are not unusual. As we proved in Atlanta, no restriction—whether a charge of trespassing or an unconstitutional city ordinance—should stand up in court.

It is worth the court hassle to prove the point. New Orleans's Mardi Gras, for example, is an annual street party where tens of thousands of people line the streets for parades. The gathering is also ripe for witnessing, since drinking and debauchery are associated with the merriment. Evangelist Scott Hinkle, whose teams have targeted that audience every year for more than a decade, reports that one thousand to fifteen hundred people accept Christ every year.

Likewise, sidewalks are strictly public and open for the practice of First Amendment rights. In Colorado Springs, Colorado, the city attorney's office issued a memorandum to arrest and prosecute street evangelists, who were known to do their lawbreaking on sidewalks. C.A.S.E. defended five criminal cases there and won all five. C.A.S.E. also obtained the right for evangelization on sidewalks surrounding public schools.

It is not appropriate to disrupt the activities inside a government building with free speech; however, the sidewalk around that building is a public forum. One group wanted to demonstrate on the sidewalk in front of the Supreme Court, but the police tried to direct them across the street. The court wisely ruled that the group was free to assemble on the sidewalk in front of the court.

Sidewalks outside of sports stadiums also are legitimate for evangelizing, though not all cities recognize this. The area around a stadium represents a tremendous opportunity to reach great numbers of people in limited periods. A stadium in a major metropolitan area draws an average of 1.8 million people in a year. These gathering places are worth fighting for, and the fights are winnable.

Beach Breach

Beaches are legal for evangelizing, too, though like Normandy Beach in World War II, you may have to fight just to set foot there.

About five hundred Christians in south Texas wanted to worship, witness and hand out tracts on the beach at South Padre Island. City officials stated in a letter that preaching the Word of God would be solicitation. Therefore, they wouldn't allow it, even though no one had planned to ask for donations. At the same time, it was widely publicized in the local newspaper that another group planned to hand out 300,000 condoms to the students who flock to the beach on spring break.

I couldn't believe the city was blocking the missionary effort. When the churches asked me to help, I said it could be handled with a phone call. So I called the city attorney and said, "Give up. You know your policy is wrong."

He said the same thing the airport commissioners said in Los Angeles: "You all threaten this every single year, and you never do anything about it."

Well, he had drawn the line in the dust. Or, in this case, the sand. So we flew to Brownsville, Texas. I stayed in an awful hotel—I mean the worst—but it didn't matter because we stayed up praying and preparing. The next morning I met with a men's prayer group and prayed some more. Churches around the whole Rio Grande Valley were praying.

In this case, the legal preparation didn't pay off. The prayer did. (I think God likes to keep us on our toes.)

I got to court, straining to sprint like a greyhound at the racetrack. "Your Honor, I'm prepared—," I said, but never got any further.

"I don't want to hear from you," said U.S. District Judge Filemon Vela. "Who represents the city?"

A slick guy, expensive suit, stands.

Vela asked, "Do you want to proceed in this case?"

"Oh, we're ready to go," he replied. "We're not going to allow this activity, your Honor."

The judge pointed to him. "Well, I'm telling you something. I'm telling you you don't want to proceed."

"What do you mean?" he asked.

"Because these Christian people have the right to evangelize on the beaches, and you don't want to proceed. Now you have twenty minutes to get a consent order worked out, or I'll issue it."

After it was over, Judge Vela turned to me and an associate, Pat Monaghan, and said, "I just want to tell you both something: God bless you."

Over one thousand people received Christ on that beach. That took place only because Christians—and I don't mean just C.A.S.E., but all those praying, witnessing people in Texas—responded to a call to action.

Shopping malls are markets open to the public. At the same time, most of them are privately owned, including the aisle space not occupied by stores. Consequently, many malls have been able to prohibit handing out tracts.

We faced that restriction when Underground Atlanta reopened with grand flourish in June 1989. In its first week of operation more than one million people visited the downtown complex of shops packed among the city's former streets and sidewalks.

Four Christians took advantage of this opportunity and handed out tracts there. They were threatened with arrest. It turned out the same development company that we had clashed with at South Street Seaport in New York—Rouse—was in control.

Rouse and the city would allow no evangelism underground or in the above-ground portion of the complex. We went to court and won the surface plaza and sidewalk and even a portion of the underground area. Had we not contested the issue, the entire complex would have been closed to the proclamation of the gospel. Once again, a willingness to test the waters, to refuse being intimidated by a giant breathing threats of illegality and arrest, opened the door for God to establish a beachhead in one of the busiest sections of downtown Atlanta.

Even though malls may prohibit you from handing out literature, no shopping center can prohibit you from wagging your tongue. If you are free to converse, you can talk about Jesus. Evangelization should proceed there. However, good training will help evangelists avoid the kinds of harassment that would rightfully upset shoppers and mall owners.

In fact, in all street evangelization, respect should be a guiding principle. Though we are called to be bold in proclaiming the gospel, it does not justify acting in a belligerent, unloving way. An improper attitude will only elicit hostility from those on the street and could be the one thing that draws an unnecessary lawsuit.

Street evangelism is not the quick-fix, ineffective ministry that some would make it. Thousands have been redeemed through ministries or campaigns of public witnessing. Many people saved on the sidewalk end up maturing in churches.

In a broad sense we are all called to street evangelism because we are all called to spread the news of redemption outside the walls of the church. All it takes to begin is a heart stirring. We must have the mind of Christ to want to share the life we have with others.

From there, church training can be helpful. How do you start a conversation with a stranger? How do you pass out a tract? The Bible stresses wisdom, and certainly evangelism is one place where wisdom reaps great dividends. Jesus said to be wise as a serpent, yet harmless as a dove. There is no better place than our public forums to put this to practice. If your church needs help in this area, C.A.S.E. can refer you to excellent ministries that specialize in training people for street evangelism. Don't pass up this tremendous opportunity for fruitfulness. These are fields ripe for harvest.

TEN

OBEYING
THE HIGHER LAW

T COULD HAVE BEEN A very expensive prayer session for Daniel.

He was well aware that King Darius had signed a law forbidding prayer to anyone but him. Violators would become chow for the lions' next meal.

Daniel probably gave very little thought to his decision to disobey the new law. Scripture says during this Babylonian captivity of the Hebrews he had been kneeling and facing Jerusalem three times a day, praying and giving thanks to God. He would continue, though there might be a price to pay.

What price should Christians be willing to pay when man's law crosses God's law? Are there cases when the Bible's commands to obey civil authority do not apply? Is there a scriptural basis for civil disobedience?

These can be difficult questions to answer. Even within the church there is disagreement. Many ministers, for example, disapprove of Operation Rescue's acts of trespass to discourage women from getting abortions. Yet many sincere Christians are willing to block abortion clinics and go to jail in order to make a visible statement about this ungodly practice and stop a few abortions in the process. Other examples of civil disobedience, directly or indirectly in the name of Christ, have emerged in recent decades: people breaking segregation laws during the civil rights movement, Christian schools and home-schooling parents resisting state certification of teachers, churches illegally harboring Central American refugees and evangelists witnessing in public places where they have been forbidden.

A Deep Tradition

Exactly what is civil disobedience? *It is the deliberate violation of an immoral law in which the violator is willing to be punished in order to draw attention to the law in hope of getting it changed.*

There is nothing new about religiously motivated civil disobedience. It can be found throughout church history, and it is well represented in the Bible. You can find stories of success, failure and mixtures of both.

Daniel, of course, ended up in the lions' den, and God brought him out alive. Earlier his three friends went into a blazing furnace for refusing to worship an idol. God vindicated them as well by sparing their lives.

Stephen's experience in Acts 6-7 turned out differently. He was brought before the Sanhedrin—a council of the Jews that had civil and criminal jurisdiction—for exercising free speech that some considered blasphemous. Instead of trying to weasel out of his mess, he launched into another speech that only inflamed his accusers more. They began gnashing their teeth. Then they stoned Stephen. He paid with his life.

One of the most detailed accounts of civil disobedience in Scripture involves Peter and the apostles in Acts 5. They had been working signs and wonders around Jerusalem when the Sadducees, jealous of their success, had them thrown into a public jail. After an angel miraculously let them out of prison, they immediately returned to the street to evangelize. They were found teaching about Christ in the temple and returned to stand before the Sanhedrin. The high priest laid out the charge:

"We gave you strict orders not to continue teaching in this name, and behold, you have filled Jerusalem with your teaching, and intend to bring this man's blood upon us" (Acts 5:28). Peter and the apostles replied, "We must obey God rather than men" (v. 29).

The Jewish council decided that it would be best to release them—though only after a good flogging and again ordering them to speak no more in Jesus' name. The apostles left, "rejoicing that they had been considered worthy to suffer shame for His name" (5:41).

And they resumed what was becoming their favorite pastime—civil disobedience through the proclamation of Jesus. _They obeyed God rather than man._

Rendering to Caesar

Daniel, Stephen and Peter heard the call to action and responded boldly. Christians today need to be equally bold, but they first must understand the full balance of what the Bible commands regarding our allegiances. Two major passages in the epistles address our proper stance before civil government. One is Romans 13:1-4:

> Let every person be in subjection to the governing authorities. For there is no authority except from God, and those which exist are established by God. Therefore he who resists authority has opposed the ordinance of God; and they who have opposed will receive condemnation upon themselves. For rulers are not a cause of fear for good behavior, but for evil. Do you want to have no fear of authority? Do what is good, and you will have praise from the same; for it is a minister of God to you for good. But if you do what is evil, be afraid; for it does not bear the sword for nothing; for it is a minister of God, an avenger who brings wrath upon the one who practices evil.

Here Paul refutes the idea that some Christians have about civil government—that because it can be perceived as an agency of secular humanism, or because it fails to prohibit abortion, it loses all authority. Under this logic the conscientious objectors obey a law within themselves, justifying the bombing of abortion clinics, the withholding of taxes or breaking any civil law they choose. But as Paul goes on to say, echoing the words of Jesus, we should render "tax to whom tax is due" (Rom. 13:7).

Peter reminded Christians that they were to submit to civil authorities and to refrain from using their freedom as an excuse for evil acts:

> Submit yourselves for the Lord's sake to every human institution, whether to a king as the one in authority, or to governors as sent by him for the punishment of evildoers and the praise of those who do right. For such is the will of God that by doing right you may silence the ignorance of foolish men.

> Act as free men, and do not use your freedom as
> a covering for evil, but use it as bondslaves of God
> (1 Pet. 2:13-16).

Christ spent much of His ministry getting under the skin of religious and secular authorities. His Sabbath healings and similar acts broke the current interpretations of Mosaic law. His proclamations of a new kingdom placed Him in subversion to the Roman rule. And it seemed as if wherever He went there arose a ruckus—disturbing the peace, as we would call it. Ditto for His disciples after His death, with their outdoor preaching and healing services.

The need for civil disobedience hardly ended with the New Testament. The late Francis Schaeffer, in his book *A Christian Manifesto*, recalled some of the Christian champions of civil disobedience.

• During a period of the Roman empire, Christians were thrown to the lions for refusing to worship Caesar.

• William Tyndale, who produced an English translation of the Bible, was executed as a heretic in 1536 because he asserted the supreme authority of the Bible over the state and the church.

• John Bunyan, author of *The Pilgrim's Progress*, three times was arrested for preaching without a state license and refusing to attend the Church of England. He spent twelve years in jail.

• John Knox, who led the Protestant Reformation in Scotland, was an outspoken critic of the Roman Catholic church. He developed a theology of resistance to tyranny, including his shocking pamphlet *Admonition to England* in 1554. His works influenced rebellions in France and Holland. He went further than other reformers, believing that common people had the duty to rebel against a government that ruled contrary to the Word of God.

Do you think these guys were concerned about their immediate predicaments? No way. They were seeing—with eyes of faith—things that most American Christians have never seen. They were cut from the same mold as the faith heroes in Hebrews 11: "All these died in faith, without receiving the promises, but having seen them and having welcomed them from a distance, and having confessed that they were strangers and exiles on the earth" (11:13). When you start thinking of your citizenship papers on file in heaven instead of in the United States of America, when you begin to take on that sojourner mentality of Abraham and Moses, the inconveniences of things like prison, even physical death, grow a little pale.

I'm not saying every Christian is duty-bound to find a corrupt civil law and defy it to the point of racking up frequent flyer points at your local jail. But let's develop eyes of faith. Let's develop ears that hear the call to action. Let's gain the spirit of Moses, who cheerfully passed up the pleasures of sin, "considering the reproach of Christ greater riches than the treasures of Egypt; for he was looking to the reward" (Heb. 11:26).

Where the Rubber Meets the Road

The basic conflict these great people of faith faced is the same issue that haunts us today: what to do when secular law does not square with the plumb line of biblical law. And in a society such as ours, where secular humanism plays an increasing role in shaping government policy and social norms, this conflict surfaces more often. The Christian's proper attitude should be that of the apostle Paul's, who said, "I also do my best to maintain always a blameless conscience both before God and before men" (Acts 24:16). Still, there come situations when one has to choose between two masters—two lawgivers—to gain that peace of conscience.

Civil authority is valid only as long as it does not overstep the authority God has given it. Lest there be any confusion about which authority supersedes the other, Paul wrote in Romans 13:1, "For there is no authority except from God."

Christian civil disobedience is perhaps best defined in the classic *Lex, Rex (The Law and the King)*, written by Samuel Rutherford in 1644. Government is sanctioned by God, he wrote, but the state is to be run according to biblical principles. When the state acts without a biblical foundation, those actions are illegitimate and therefore acts of tyranny. A tyrannical government is immoral, he argued, and consequently a satanic entity. Therefore, *it is not only the right but the duty of Christians to resist such governments.* To do otherwise is to resist God.

Sometimes that first step of resistance takes the form of civil disobedience. Many of the situations C.A.S.E. has tackled involved Christians who evangelized where they were not supposed to—at least according to someone's interpretation of the law. Sometimes the evangelists stopped after being threatened with arrest. Sometimes they ended up behind bars.

That's what happened in Oakland, California. On July 14, 1987, seven Christians were arrested by security guards for distributing gospel tracts on the sidewalk outside the Oakland Coliseum. Two of the seven were charged with criminal trespass and put in jail. By January 29, 1988, C.A.S.E. got the judge to drop the criminal charges.

We spent months trying to negotiate with the city of Oakland to have the regulations changed concerning First Amendment activities around the coliseum. We failed with education, so we turned to litigation. On June 13, 1988, a district court declared the city's regulation unconstitutional.

Five days later some of the original Christians who were

arrested returned to the scene of the crime to share the gospel news. One of the security guards who made the arrests accepted Jesus that day!

There are also forms of free speech that are controversial yet protected by law, so they are not acts of civil disobedience. For example, Christians assembled in protests across the nation when the movie *The Last Temptation of Christ* was released. These were people who understood that the film gave a blasphemous, inaccurate portrayal of Christ, including a sexual fantasy in His dying moments. Just because filmmakers have the right to produce weird, offensive works doesn't mean we have to sit around and passively accept it. Those who marched in protest near theaters were simply exercising basic rights.

Were a judge to issue a restraining order, saying there were too many people in front of a given theater, the situation would change. The protesters would have to decide if they wanted to risk arrest to protest both the movie and a judicial action they might perceive as unconstitutional.

Each situation needs to be evaluated on its own merits. Ecclesiastes 3:8 tells us there is a time for war and a time for peace. We should maintain the stance Paul expressed, that he would do things by the leading of the Holy Spirit. In considering a protest of *Last Temptation,* for example, a balancing factor would be to consider that the freedom that gives movie producers license to make whatever they want is the same freedom that gives Christians a chance to publish and broadcast what they want and to protest without retribution.

Willing to Pay the Price

Perhaps the person most remembered for civil disobedience in the twentieth century is Mahatma Gandhi. He is known for his experiments with nonviolence to bring about change. For example, he organized a strike among Indian miners during his twenty-one-year stay in South Africa, where he was working to improve the rights of Indians. After he returned to India, he used techniques such as fasting to draw attention to the plight of the oppressed. He would tell his followers that *you must make the price you pay so great that society is not willing to watch you pay it.*

The price is not always legal, rational punishment but a backlash of unjustified force. When Rosa Parks refused to give up her bus seat to a white man in Alabama, it was a nonviolent act, but it mushroomed into an entire movement which often was met with violence. Though Martin Luther King and other civil rights leaders employed marches, prayer vigils and other nonviolent actions, as espoused by Gandhi, they too often were met with brutality, even death, by police and private citizens who resisted their pleas for change.

Civil disobedience is scriptural. It can work. It doesn't always work quickly, as the civil rights movement illustrates, but it is encouraging to see those first cracks appearing in the bastions of evil.

Someone protesting in front of an abortion clinic once told me of a potential client who decided against having an abortion. The woman said that when she saw there were strangers willing to get arrested for her and her baby, she realized there was a true love there. And this is scriptural: We are to be known by our love for one another. When Christians in this way can get the hearts of people attuned to God's perspective on a certain issue, the battle can be won before the law ever changes.

If civil rights for blacks was the civil disobedience battleground of the 1960s, civil rights for the unborn is the hotbed for civil disobedience in the 1990s. In the next chapter we will look at how abortion stacks up against the criteria for civil obedience. There's plenty of work to be done on this front. God has granted many victories already, and I believe there are bigger ones to come.

ELEVEN

PRO-LIFE
LAWBREAKERS

CANNOT IN GOOD conscience pay that fine."

With those words, Operation Rescue leader Randall Terry turned down a deal from Fulton County state Judge John Bruner. The judge offered to suspend a two-year prison sentence if Terry would pay a $500 fine and agree to stay out of the Atlanta area for two years.

I could not believe Terry's act of minor civil disobedience had come to this. He was charged with unlawful assembly and trespassing at an abortion clinic as part of a mass rally to protest abortion during the Democratic National Convention in Atlanta. Though he was technically representing himself in court, I was coaching him before Judge Bruner.

I knew Terry had been found not guilty on all counts when he was tried on similar charges in Los Angeles. Furthermore, in a unanimous opinion involving participants in the same

Atlanta rescue incident, the Georgia Court of Appeals held that the people blocking the doors to the clinic could not be found guilty of both trespass and unlawful assembly at the same time. On this basis, I thought surely Terry would be entitled to a mistrial.

I asked Bruner to apply that decision. He refused. I pleaded, showing him the case rules, until the bailiff asked me to sit down. In a travesty that easily merits an appeal, the judge never even allowed Terry to present his defense, yet the jury found him guilty. He began serving his two-year term, but he was released after four and a half months when someone anonymously paid the fine.

"We Did Not Know This"

What motivates a man like Randall Terry to commit acts that reward him with a prison term? What strengthens his conscience to the point that he would resist paying a fine when it means being separated from his wife and children for two years? For one thing, Terry and the hundreds who have followed him to block abortuaries in Atlanta and many other cities have a keen sense of the gross injustice of abortion *and* they want to act on this burden. They do not want to have to stand before God and feign dullness to the evil that surrounds us. Proverbs 24:11-12 warns:

> Deliver those who are being taken away to death,
> And those who are staggering to slaughter,
> O hold them back.
> If you say, "See, we did not know this,"
> Does He not consider it who weighs the hearts?

Those who refuse to acknowledge that the unborn "are being taken away to death" argue that they only want to give women a right of "choice." By this they mean they want the individual to be a law unto herself, to determine what's right and what's wrong. This kind of ethics meshes with secular humanism, holding that man is the measure of all things. It says man reserves the last word on every "choice" in life. It will not acknowledge moral absolutes that predetermine certain choices, such as the morality of killing unborn children.

In short, abortion presents a classic example of where man's law butts heads with God's law. As we saw in the last chapter, this is the formula for Christian civil disobedience. The Bible prohibits murder, and this is the primary issue when you deal with the morality of abortion.

Before examining civil disobedience regarding abortion, let's review the biblical, medical and legal aspects involved with taking the life of the unborn.

God's Handiwork

Abortionists would like everyone to believe that life begins upon birth. Not a moment sooner. Yet the Bible takes a much broader view of God's marvelous creation process:

"Now the word of the Lord came to me saying, 'Before I formed you in the womb I knew you, and before you were born I consecrated you' " (Jer. 1:4-5).

"For Thou didst form my inward parts; Thou didst weave me in my mother's womb. I will give thanks to Thee, for I am fearfully and wonderfully made" (Ps. 139:13-14).

Luke 1 illustrates life in the unborn. When Mary, pregnant with Jesus, went to visit Elizabeth, her unborn son, John the Baptist, leaped in the womb for joy at Mary's greeting. An earlier prophecy (Luke 1:15) had said Elizabeth's baby would be filled with the Holy Spirit while he was still in the womb.

Dictionaries define abortion as the termination or premature expulsion of offspring. The "offspring" of a man and woman is a person. At the moment of conception, twenty-three chromosomes from the mother merge with twenty-three chromosomes from the father to form a unique person. When the fetus is eighteen weeks old, it weighs three-quarters of a pound, has a nose, lips, hands and fingers, and ears. It can move and respond to touch. Yet four hundred children at this age or older are killed daily by abortion in the United States.

Property or Person?

Abortionists, desperate to justify their position, have argued that the fetus is not viable outside of the womb until it is near its full term. However, the idea of "viability" as a basis for allowing some or all abortions is bogus.

First, with advances in medical science, babies as young as five months after conception have been able to survive outside the womb. But, more important, viability is an arbitrary concept. Even babies born after full term will die unless they receive the mother's milk or similar nourishment provided by an adult. They are completely dependent upon the mother, as is an eight-month-old fetus, which is normally viable outside the womb, and an eight-week-old fetus, which is not.

Viability is arbitrary in part because tests other than survival could be applied with equal logic, especially after birth. For example, babies that demonstrate some measure of mental retardation or physical defects could be killed. Extremists in the secular humanist camp have already proposed such screening of life. Does this smack of the Nazi-like logic that only certain lives are worth living? You bet.

Legally, the rights of the unborn have much in common with last century's denial of rights to blacks. In the Dred Scott decision of 1857 the Supreme Court declared that no black—free or slave—could claim United States citizenship. Black slaves were found to be property. Because slaves were legally property and not citizens, or people, killing them would not be grounds for homicide in a court of law. As long as abortionists can define the fetus as something less than a person, they have a chance of perpetuating the right to kill it.

The unborn enjoyed good legal protection before the Supreme Court's *Roe v. Wade* decision in 1973. All fifty states had laws prohibiting abortion until then. But a majority of a nine-member court, in one collective stroke, declared it knew how to interpret the U.S. Constitution better than the legislatures of every state. It conveniently discerned in the "penumbra" (shadow) of the Constitution a right to privacy and then shoehorned it into the abortion dilemma.

While the court's majority was busy finding phantoms in the shadows, it ignored an explicit statement of rights found in the Declaration of Independence: "We hold these truths to be self-evident, that all men are created equal, that they are endowed by their Creator with certain unalienable rights, that among these are life, liberty and the pursuit of happiness." The nation's founders recognized what a modern court did not: that the creation of life is a divine act, not just a sex act, and that *all* human life has *an unalienable right* to thrive.

Because the court could not define, to its own satisfaction, when life begins, it came up with arbitrary divisions of pregnancy. Up to three months in the womb, the child can be aborted without restrictions. From three months to six months, the states may make laws on where and how abortions can be done but cannot prohibit abortions. After six months, the states can stop abortions, but not if the mother's physical or mental health might be endangered. Even the final trimester restriction is so vague that it has resulted in abortion on demand throughout the country.

Roe, twisting constitutional rights and common sense as it did, has produced a virtual schizophrenia of law. For example, hospitals and doctors have successfully obtained court orders when it was determined that a Caesarean birth was necessary to best protect the life of a child. Or when it is known an unborn child needs a blood transfusion to remain alive, blood cannot be denied to the child. Yet the same legal framework that demands these life-sustaining measures allows deliberate killing of a child.

Since *Roe*, states have tried to institute various measures to put restrictions on abortion that, in light of the breadth allowed by the Supreme Court, would be relatively minor. These include parental notification laws, requiring that one or sometimes two parents be informed of a planned abortion by a minor child; or spousal notification, to let the father know. Most of these laws have been struck down. Also found unconstitutional have been more restrictive measures, where states have tried to limit abortion to cases such as where the mother's life is in danger, or where there is proof the infant will be handicapped.

The main legal breakthrough has been the Supreme Court's *Webster v. Reproductive Health Services* decision in 1989. This opened the door for states to pass their own restrictions on abortion. We've yet to see how far they will go, if they go anywhere at all, in the direction of protecting the unborn. Much damage was done in the sixteen years that *Roe* ruled without question. Public opinion has become much more tolerant of abortion; an entire generation has grown up thinking abortion rights were etched in the tablets on Mount Sinai. The pro-abortion side is well-organized and well-funded and has demonstrated it will not willingly give way to the slightest restriction that would curtail abortion rights as they now stand.

Most observers expect that the best that pro-lifers can expect in the legislative arena for the next few years is compromise in some states. While this would be welcome in one sense—even minor restrictions could save the lives of thousands of babies per year—it would still leave us a nation that condones the shedding of innocent blood. So even with piecemeal victories in some states, Christian civil disobedience will be a major tactic to be considered in the fight to halt abortion in the 1990s.

To Retreat or to Rescue

It was the Gideon Project. Like the Old Testament character Gideon, Matthew Goldsby and James Simmons felt God had told them to go on a mission of destruction. Whereas Gideon was told to destroy pagan altars, Goldsby and Simmons felt led to destroy an abortion clinic and the offices of two gynecologists who had performed abortions.

After their homemade pipe bombs blew up early Christmas morning 1984, Goldsby's fiancee, Kaye Wiggins, called it "a gift to Jesus on His birthday." A jury in Pensacola, Florida, called it lawlessness.

The jurors were right. The two young men deserved punishment, and they got it: ten years in prison with five years of probation and an order to pay $353,073 each in restitution to the two gynecologists.

This incident and others before it made for an unfortunate start of the Christian resistance to abortion clinics through civil disobedience. By the time the Gideon Project made headlines, hundreds of incidents of threats, vandalism and bombing directed at abortion clinics and their personnel had been reported. These tactics accomplished little for the pro-life side.

Yet much was accomplished for the pro-abortion side. Abortionists, for promotional purposes, continue to lump together all resistance to clinics as extremist violence. For example, a 1989 Planned Parenthood advertisement says pro-lifers are "attacking the Constitution...and when they don't get their way, they resort to threats and violence."

There are anti-abortion acts of civil disobedience that do not involve threats or violence to people or property. The most publicized effort of recent years has been Operation Rescue. Participants in Operation Rescue have simply chosen to place their bodies between the abortionist and his victims: the women and babies. Faced with honoring two laws—"Do not trespass" and "Do not murder"—they choose to support the higher law.

This is consistent with general application of law. If you see someone drowning in a pool surrounded by a fence with "No Trespassing" signs, you are entitled to jump the fence in order to save the life without fear of prosecution for trespassing. This is called the necessity defense. The rescuers are literally out to save lives, in addition to making a statement.

Operation Rescue and similar sit-ins may not have permanently closed any clinics. But by shutting them for a day or several hours, some of the potential clients were delayed, and some went home and decided against abortion. Many cases are known where clients talked with protesters and then decided against the abortion.

Michael Hirsh, who organized rescues in Atlanta, tells of a jail guard who was planning to abort twins. As a result of talking with the arrested pro-lifers, she decided against the abortion. Arrested protesters also were able to counsel pregnant inmates against having abortions and in some cases toward a saving knowledge of Christ.

And there is potential for even greater effect. Suppose in

a major city like Atlanta there was an outpouring of thousands of people to block clinics—more people than could be carted away for arrest. Not only would clinics be closed during that time, but state legislators as well as members of Congress would take serious notice. This is one form of voting that takes place outside the ballot box and does not have to wait for election day.

Other Strategies

Operation Rescue is certainly one of the most dramatic and newsworthy techniques for battling abortion. In the long run it may prove to be one of the most effective. But there are similar approaches that do not always constitute civil disobedience.

In late 1989 a group of Christian organizations planned a mass anti-abortion gathering in Washington, D.C., called the D.C. Project. They signed contracts for use of an armory and an auditorium and talked with police about coordinating outdoor activities. These included preaching, distributing tracts and picketing abortion clinics.

Everything seemed fine until a lawsuit was filed against the D.C. Project by the National Organization for Women. I happened to be in Washington and teamed up with three other lawyers with whom I'd worked in the past. NOW attacked the pro-life aspect of the project. They attacked the free speech activities. They were represented by one of Washington's biggest law firms, but somebody forgot to tell God, who was busy putting into His servants' slingshot a smooth little stone. NOW took it on the forehead; they did not obtain the type of relief they wanted.

While we were praising God for the victory, NOW filed two more lawsuits, in Virginia and Maryland. They asked the courts to overrule the Washington decision by Judge Louis

F. Oberdorfer, who refused to issue the type of injunction against the pro-life activities that NOW desired. We plunged ahead with work, staying up until 3:00 A.M. for four days. NOW failed again in both states.

Still there was more resistance. The Washington City Council tried to thwart Judge Oberdorfer's ruling by passing an emergency order to block the D.C. Project. "Emergency order" meant they could circumvent the normal public hearing process and by fiat crush our First Amendment freedoms of free speech and assembly. We countered by successfully filing for a preliminary injunction. The D.C. Project proceeded at last.

I'm not trying to brag that we were Superlawyers or that we have the endurance of marathoners. I simply want to show that these things can be won. If God is for us, it doesn't matter who's against us. Or how long it takes.

Abortion protests also can be conducted on a much smaller scale than the D.C. Project. While many people cannot or will not risk arrest at clinics, they can still be effective near the clinics by passing out leaflets giving a realistic perspective on abortion. If the distribution is done on public property, there is no risk of arrest for trespassing.

Then there is always the prospect of picketing—in front of the abortion mills, in front of the homes of abortionists, or the homes of legislators or city council members who vote for abortion rights, in front of media outlets that editorialize in favor of abortion. Organizing and participating in boycotts, when a business or an advertiser has a clear tie to the support of abortion rights, can be effective, as it has been in the fight against pornography.

We must continue to call and write members of Congress to let them know our concerns about abortion. Especially in light of the *Webster* decision, we need to communicate with our governors and state legislatures. We should write letters to the editors of newspapers and magazines.

Furthermore, unwed mothers, both those who choose to keep their babies and those who give them up for adoption, need help. Many of those who seek abortions are twelve to eighteen years old. They are confused and grappling with guilt. They are suffering from the emotional pressure of dealing with their boyfriends and their own families. Taking into your home such young women who need a temporary shelter can be the finest example of a faith that proves itself with works. What most of these women need is salvation, compassion and forgiveness. A loving relationship in a home environment can be the best way to begin or nurture that new life in Christ.

Those who cannot open their homes in this way can participate in much of the same ministry by counseling or other work through their local abortion alternative center, such as Birthright or Sav-A-Life.

There are always opportunities to work through elected representatives at the state and national level and sometimes at the local level. One national goal would be to have a constitutional amendment that would declare life begins at conception. From there, abortion could be classed with all statutes related to homicide.

Most important, Christians must pray. Prayer is the most potent method for changing laws, for changing the hearts and minds of women and those who participate in the abortion industry, as well as the young men who are so irresponsible with their sexual behavior. Prayer can also give you the personal guidance necessary to make the best investment of your time and energy to fight this national scourge.

The contrast between man's law and God's law is striking enough to justify civil disobedience in the area of abortion, but violating the law is not the only response in this call to action. I encourage you to seek God about finding a place to join the ranks in this struggle.

PORNOGRAPHY: ABUSING THE FREEDOM OF EXPRESSION

I F YOU DOUBT THAT Satan is a master deceiver, look at the fun he's had with the First Amendment to the U.S. Constitution.

As we've seen, the opponents of religion have perverted to their own ends the First Amendment's carefully phrased protection of free religious expression. As a result most Americans mindlessly tolerate school personnel who persecute the mildest Christian expression. If a city ordinance bans free religious speech in public places, no big deal.

Now, adding insult to injury, *those who would throw off all moral restraint have used the First Amendment's protection of free speech to justify the production and sale of the most vile and violent pornography to anyone who wants it, anywhere, any time.*

Once again the church has been hard of hearing when the

145

call to action went out. Too many Christians think the battle for pornography is nothing more than getting the local convenience store to put *Penthouse* and *Hustler* magazines in brown wrappers behind the counter. True, these small battles must be fought, and they are by no means easy. But these so-called "soft-core pornography" magazines represent only the transition to a much darker realm. In this vast underworld smut dealers are trafficking in clear-cut crime, virtually enslaving women and children and activating the most hideous tendencies in potentially criminal minds. And all this under the banner of freedom of speech.

Pornography's Underbelly

Those who've specialized in the fight against pornography tell of a common problem. Christians, who should be the most militant adversaries of pornography, don't fully understand what it is they are called to fight.

If they knew well their Old Testament, they would have a good idea. They would know not only the depth of depravity at issue, but also that they should be on the lookout for manifestations of immorality because there is nothing new under the sun. Leviticus 19 gives explicit commands against incest, adultery, bestiality and child sacrifice—some of the favorite themes of today's pornography.

Unfortunately, when Christians make church presentations on the subject, they cannot show slides drawn from typical hard-core pornography. They cannot discreetly show images of a girl coupling with a German shepherd. They cannot display police photographs of the bodies of women who have been raped and mutilated by men fueled with filth. Consequently, some Christians question whether anti-porn fighters are simply modern-day Victorians unappreciative of God's marvelous creations of the human body and sex. That they would even raise the question shows how vastly they underestimate the seriousness of this issue.

The opportunists who cater to America's demand for "adult" products have created a $4 billion a year industry. Their products do more than simply stretch the limits of network television, where bare breasts in prime time may represent the cutting edge of controversy. For years, pornography has been portraying through magazines, books and movies (now in inexpensive, easily available videotapes) the most unorthodox scenes of sex and violence one could ever fantasize. Even in communities that forbid the sale of such prurient material, consumers can always obtain it through the mail.

In the context of the decay of religious freedoms in the United States, there are at least three major concerns with this unrestricted market in pornography. The first is slavery.

Our schools teach that slavery ended with President Lincoln's Emancipation Proclamation more than one hundred years ago. While slavery may have ceased for blacks, a more insidious form of slavery has arisen this century for women and children.

One of the chief aspects of our nation's early slave trade was that it treated human beings as nothing more than property. Because they had no rights, they were degraded. They were, in effect, sub-human. Perhaps more than the poverty and cruelty to which blacks were subjected, this blow to their spirits—an overwhelming sense of worthlessness, of being made in the image of animal, not God, of lacking a basic God-given integrity—was the most demeaning aspect.

Slavery has again entered society through the back door of human lust. Because pornography divorces sex from marriage, from commitment, even from love, it reduces its models to performing animals. They are not artists; they are not even actors or actresses. They are simply performers in the most elementary sense of the word. Like the Negro slaves, they evidence no humanness.

And once the models become trapped by pornography's world of easy money, drugs and underworld characters, they find it as difficult to escape as did the black slaves of the nineteenth century. Many never escape. For some of pornography's slaves, their careers end face down in an alley, or lying in a bed, dead from a drug overdose, or wasting away in a hospital bed as AIDS ravages their bodies.

Even more pathetic is the enslavement of children into this nightmare. Unlike the men and women who choose this lifestyle, hundreds of thousands of children have been pushed into modeling for this criminal world of exploitation before they even understand it.

This brings us to a second abuse of freedom. While many argue that there may be borderline cases where soft-core pornography merits a certain amount of free speech protection under the First Amendment, the hard-core porn industry merits nothing but prosecution because it is built on criminal activity. Child pornography, for example, depicts the rape or sodomization of a child, which is illegal. And for all the liberalization of sex our society tolerates, prostitution remains a crime in most all cities and states. Yet prostitution—sex for pay—is regularly engaged in by those who participate in the porn industry. Bestiality as well is unlawful almost everywhere, though it remains a favorite subject for pornographers to traffick in.

Where's the Beef?

A third major attack pornography wages on our freedom is outright violence. Civil libertarians are fond of claiming that pornography has no victims. As we've seen, pornography already claims too many victims—the hundreds of thousands of women, men and children whose lives are ruined emotionally, spiritually and often physically by the numbing abuse of serving as sex objects.

Tragically, there are millions more who are victims. They are the consumers who become desensitized, dehumanized like the players in the porn industry. And, most tragically, a small but significant portion of society becomes innocent victims when men inflamed by smut-fed passions rape and murder at random.

One such consumer who became a victim and who in turn victimized others was Ted Bundy. He was convicted of murdering a twelve-year-old girl and is believed to have murdered dozens of women across the United States. On January 23, 1989, the day before his execution, Bundy explained to James Dobson, head of Focus on the Family ministry, the devious role pornography played in his life.

"I'm not blaming pornography. I'm not saying that it caused me to go out and do certain things," Bundy said in the videotaped interview. "The issue is how this kind of literature contributed and helped mold and shape the kinds of violent behavior." Bundy explained the addictive nature of his indulgence. Like heroin, pornography stimulated a swelling demand that could be satisfied only by more potent indulgences. Finally, Bundy realized that pornography could take him only so far. The next step would be to cross into reality. So he did. Then he discovered that one act of sexual violence would satisfy only for a time. He became a slave to the repetition of his real-life pornographic fantasies.

"I've lived in prison for a long time now," he said, "and I've met a lot of men who were motivated to commit violence just like me. And without exception every one of them was deeply involved in pornography, without question, without exception, deeply influenced and consumed by an addiction to pornography.''

Bundy's conclusion from his prison acquaintances has been borne out by formal studies. An FBI study of 1985 of thirty-six serial murderers showed that 81 percent said pornography was one of their highest sexual interests.[1] In another study 86 percent of rapists admitted regular use of pornography.[2] A Michigan State Police study of thirty-eight thousand sex crimes over twenty years showed pornography was related to 41 percent of the acts.[3]

The Bible also links sexual obsessions with violence and other sins. Murder and strife are among the sins listed in Romans 1 following Paul's warning against homosexuality. Galatians 5 begins a sin list with ''immorality, impurity, sensuality'' in verse 19. It continues with ''idolatry, sorcery, enmities, strife, jealousy, outbursts of anger'' and other transgressions. James 1:14-15 outlines the process clearly: ''But each one is tempted when he is carried away and enticed by his own lust. Then when lust has conceived, it gives birth to sin; and when sin is accomplished, it brings forth death.''

This principle applies not only to spiritual death but, in the case of pornography, to physical death. Allen Sears of the Children's Legal Foundation tells of specific cases that illustrate the connection. Telephone pornography—so-called ''dial-a-porn''—hooked a Baptist deacon in California. After filling his mind and spirit with hours of this audial stimulation, he raped and murdered a nine-year-old girl.

In Wassau, Wisconsin, a man obsessed with pornography killed his sister-in-law. He reportedly was involved with acts of cannibalism with the corpse.

A man in Phoenix, Arizona, was sentenced to 320 years in prison for serial rapes. This man told how he practically lived in adult stores, watching peep shows for hours.

Eventually he sought victims who looked like the victims in the movies. After all, he rationalized to himself in a myth common to pornographic movies, even if the women resisted, they would actually enjoy what he would do to them.

Pornography, then, is not a victimless crime. From the women and innocent children who are ensnared into producing this hideous world of perversion, to the men who become addicted to its titillation, to the innocent women who are raped and killed, there are countless victims. With something of this magnitude, not only individuals but society as well is victimized by a lowered moral consensus. Author William Stanmeyer has written:

> Though crude, pornography is a philosophical statement. It says: there are no rules about sex; sex is trivial; sex is for entertainment. Though debased, pornography is a theological statement. It says: there is no God who says I should limit my lust or channel my passion or give as well as get...pornography is anti-woman and anti-child. It is anti-marriage and anti-permanence. Thus it is profoundly anti-civilization. Since civilization is social support to the dynamics of life, pornography is anti-life.[4]

Pornography's Proselytizers

Perhaps your town has never been traumatized by a serial rapist or killer. Maybe you are fortunate enough to live where there are no adult bookstores or theaters. Pornography may seem more like a problem for cities such as Los Angeles, where much of this seedy filth is produced and consumed.

Yet pornography in some form threatens everyone, especially families with children. The average child in America watches one hundred R-rated movies a year, thanks largely to the proliferation of cable TV stations and video rentals. That same access also means that a deluge of other unrated films, often the equivalent of X-rated, can be seen in one's home by youngsters.

While the typical first-run movies that compete for Oscars may have no more than your familiar dose of sex, profanity and violence—usually too much as it is for the R and PG-13 productions—the cinema output as a whole is much worse. In the movie *Nightmare* a woman's head was severed from her body while she had sex. In *Blood Feast* a woman had her tongue pulled out while she was being raped. Author Phil Phillips, citing the National Coalition Against Television Violence, said that in 1987 one of six Hollywood movies contained a violent rape scene.[5]

Do not presume that your teenage son is immune to this stuff. The porn-saturated rapists and murderers may get all the media attention, but they are not pornography's biggest market. *The largest consumers of hard-core pornography are children twelve to seventeen years old.* This is partly because of the nature of teenagers. While adults are generally ashamed of their interest in pornography, boys have a different perspective. Often rebellious, inquisitive and aggressive by nature, teenage boys are quick to show their explicit treasures to their friends.

A University of Houston study examined the level of exposure to pornography for junior high and high school students. Not a single boy was found who hadn't seen issues of *Penthouse* or *Playboy* magazines. For exposure to hard-core porn, the figure was around 80 percent.

Needless to say, teens are quite impressionable. They are still forming identities about themselves and figuring out how to relate to the opposite sex. If we allow them to base their sexual identity on pornography, we can expect the worst from them as adults.

And even when they have had good values inculcated at home, this is no guarantee. A study in the 1950s cited by Phillips showed that people could be shown a movie portraying values different from their own and consequently experience a radical change in their own value system.[6]

The Weight of Heavy Metal

Teens' development is also threatened by exposure to the violent, sexually explicit lyrics that come from a handful of raunchy heavy-metal rock bands. Some of these groups draw a big portion of their audience from ten- to thirteen-year-olds. These youngsters do not need to hear Guns 'n' Roses singing about cutting off a girl's breasts and then subjecting her to intercourse and sodomy. As we will see in chapter 14's review of satanism, musicians such as Ozzy Osbourne suggest extreme violence, including suicide. Many teens have followed up on the offer.

Once again libertarians use the First Amendment's free speech protection to defend this garbage. They have resisted attempts to unmask the minority of rock music that propagates these dangerously suggestive lyrics.

Tipper Gore, wife of Tennessee senator Albert Gore, and her Parents' Music Resource Center have proposed a simple labeling system to alert parents to the nature of the music their kids bring home. The tag would state "Explicit Lyrics—Parental Advisory." A much more elaborate rating system has worked for years with movies, but the rock music industry cannot imagine submitting to this proposal.

The critics call it censorship. They're wrong. According to the *American Heritage Dictionary,* censorship is *prohibiting* something objectionable. What's proposed for rock music is simply providing information for consumers who genuinely need it. If I buy a can of soup, I don't have to guess what's inside or send it down to a lab once I open it at home. Instead, the label tells me in detail what I have a right to know. Rock star Frank Zappa has protested that some people would not buy records if they had a warning label.

Of course, the goal is not to pull the plug on the rock music industry. The primary concern is to protect parents and their impressionable children. A system such as this would in no way jeopardize First Amendment freedom.

Porn-free

Christians enjoy much stronger legal support when it comes to the more traditional forms of pornography—magazines and movies. Libertarians can prattle on about their rights to free expression, but when it comes to pornography there are sound ground rules already established by the courts. Not even soft-core porn is completely protected in the way it can be sold. Communities can require that magazine covers be wrapped in brown paper. The location of porn newsracks and stores can be zoned to certain areas. And, better than that, you can even chase the smut pushers straight out of town.

In Southern California a Catholic archbishop organized an interdenominational group of pastors. They began to educate their people about the trash being carried by video stores. Each Sunday the pastors handed out lists of stores that carried no pornographic videos and encouraged their folks to do business only with them. They called it selective shopping. The flip side of the coin is that it's a boycott against certain other stores. However you look at it, it's perfectly legal. Now entire cities in Southern California are porn-free. Nationwide, more than forty communities are free of pornography.

Unlike abortion, where Christians may find themselves in

a minority, pornography enjoys about as much prestige among Americans as Iran did during the hostage crisis. Polls show three out of four Americans want the government to crack down more on pornography. And for kiddie porn, 94 percent want tougher restrictions. Most feminists detest pornography because it degrades women. Civic-minded people who may not be religious don't like pornography because an influx of adult stores is a sure way to cripple a neighborhood.

There are many ways to fight smut. In addition to boycotting local stores, citizens can urge newspapers and magazines simply to reject advertising of blatantly pornographic goods or services. Citizens can examine their local zoning codes and see how adult stores or the sale of adult items can be restricted to certain neighborhoods.

Citizens also can boycott national consumer goods producers who advertise on risque television shows or in distasteful magazines. Michigan housewife Terry Rakolta, with her letter-writing campaign, affected network television. She complained that the Fox network sitcom "Married...With Children" was offensive. As a result, major advertisers such as Kimberly-Clark and Procter & Gamble said they planned to run no more ads on the show due to its content. Tambrands, maker of Tampax, canceled a commercial.

Not every batch of letters is going to get the same results as achieved by Mrs. Rakolta, a socialite who sits on the boards of cultural and charitable institutions and apparently had some degree of clout to accompany her letters. Still, God delights in turning odds topsy-turvy.

Also there is strength in coalitions. About sixteen hundred Christian leaders formed CLeaR-TV (Christian Leaders for Responsible Television). The group notified television sponsors that they would begin monitoring shows in 1989 and that boycotts would follow. Secular critics rant about this being censorship, but it's no such thing. Nobody is compelled to do business with companies whose advertising supports programs that encourage sexual immorality and ridicule religion and traditional values.

I would be presumptuous not to add that foremost we must be diligent to protect our own temple. We must consecrate our eyes, ears and mind to the purposes of God. We are commanded to take every thought captive to Christ. It's sad but true that Christians are by no means immune to the magnetic lure of pornography. No one of us can be an effective warrior for our community if we have already been defeated within.

Satan's legions have got the jump on us in this area. They have perverted the precious guarantees of freedom found in our nation's First Amendment. The broad result has been diminished freedom of religious expression while expressions of immorality enjoy increased freedom.

It's been said that all it takes for evil to flourish is for righteous people to do nothing. Evil, in the form of pornography, continues to thrive in most American communities because the righteous people in those cities are doing nothing, or next to nothing. This war is full of battles begging to be fought. And most of them can be won with little or no compromise because there is such strong public sentiment against pornography. Make your community one of those that rises up in anger to halt the flow of filth inside its borders.

NEW AGE, OLD LIE

THE ATLANTA GROCERY owner knew his life had been changed for the better.

This conversion, though, had nothing to do with the gospel of Jesus Christ. It came through a program called The Forum. This was a 1980s version of Werner Erhard's est (Erhard Seminar Training), one of the best known of the human potential movement's expensive courses.

Problem was, the owner of DeKalb Farmers' Market felt strongly—too strongly—that it could also change the lives of his employees. He began to coerce some of them to attend, in some cases at a cost of five hundred dollars. If they balked, they faced termination.

DeKalb Farmers' Market was large, so its employees represented a broad spectrum of religions—Baptist, Presbyterian, Jewish, Jehovah's Witnesses and Hindu. Many of them had been with the business for years, helping it grow. Yet some of these loyal employees lost their jobs because their religious convictions would not allow them to submit to this self-improvement course. Their reason: they felt it would compromise their religious convictions.

Were they correct? Unquestionably. Not just The Forum and est, but a panorama of beliefs and religions loosely grouped under the tag New Age are propagating practices and philosophies directly at odds with Christianity.

The grocery's employees stood up for their rights and took legal action. They eventually received a very successful settlement, including a provision that they not be coerced into any kind of program. Others are not as lucky. In some of the highest levels of the business world New Age material is turning up as motivational courses that flirt with the supernatural. It's invading education as teaching techniques that also dabble in the otherworldly. It's in sports, in medicine—you name it.

This penetration should sound alarms in the hearts of Christians. As we've seen with secular humanism, when you remove the principles and presence of Christianity from any institution, you will find another morality emerging, however subtle it may appear on the surface.

No one has to submit to any kind of job training with a spiritual bent to it—be it yoga or transcendental meditation, whether or not it's identified with the New Age movement. That doesn't mean some employer or teacher won't try to get away with it. When they do try, as they have in Atlanta and elsewhere, they're threatening our religious freedom. We shouldn't tolerate it for a minute.

Aquarius and More

The term New Age derives from the coming of the Age

of Aquarius, a popular theme and song of the 1960s. The first hints of a new age emerged around the turn of the century. Afrikaner "prophet" Johanna Brandt's books in the early 1900s spoke of the "dawning of the Age of Aquarius." The concept stems from astrological theory in which there are "star ages." This theory has it that for the past two thousand years Earth has been influenced by Pisces, the astrological fish sign. This sign is linked with Christianity, because early Christians adopted the sign.

Astrologers cannot pin down when the Age of Pisces ends, but they agree we are on the verge of the Aquarian Age, possibly already in it. The Age of Aquarius is supposed to be marked by humanism, brotherhood and occult happenings.

In addition to the movements already mentioned, the New Age umbrella incorporates astrology, reincarnation, channeling, the occult, hauntings, ghosts, UFOs, ESP (extrasensory perception), pantheism (equating God with the forces of nature), animism (attributing conscious life to nature or natural objects) and other beliefs.

New Age philosophies deny the existence of a personal God who loves His own. They exalt human potential and scientific progress. They corrupt Christianity and other established religions, borrowing a few terms and concepts but never lining up with them.

The New Age touches on Christianity with its vague belief that God is in each person. But why stop there? It also believes God is in rocks, trees—you name it. If this sounds confusing, well, it is. Loosey-goosey New Age tolerates a hodgepodge of religions.

Yet the New Age god presumed to be so ever-present has left no absolute law, as we know the Bible to be. New Agers, finding God in themselves, make up their law as they go. In this sense New Age is no different from secular humanism.

Man is the measure of himself. Satan's same deception that disturbed the peace in the Garden of Eden reigns: "You shall be as gods."

Actress Shirley MacLaine, one of New Age's best known gurus, is quite blunt about self-deification: "I know that I exist, therefore I AM. I know the God-source exists. Therefore IT IS. Since I am part of that force, then I AM that I AM." Sound a bit like the name Jehovah used before Moses? It's no accident.

Taking it further, it's been said that New Age is Satan's counterfeit of the prophesied millennium. The peace and harmony that the Bible promises of the millennium are forecast by New Agers as the Age of Aquarius, an era of world peace and prosperity.

For example, Maharishi Mahesh Yogi, who popularized transcendental meditation in the United States in the 1970s, greeted the dawning of the 1990s with a press release titled "Maharishi Offers Heaven on Earth to Every Government." It explained that he perceived recent world events, such as the move for freedom in Eastern Europe, as "a phase transition from an age of ignorance to the Age of Enlightenment." The Maharishi invited "major bankers and the governments of wealthy nations" to invest in his projects. Among these are his schools, the "Maharishi Cities of Immortals," and the "Maharishi Electric Car, a state-of-the-art automobile being built by the Electric Chariot Division of Maharishi Heaven on Earth Development Corporation."

Only a handful of Westerners is willing to sign on the dotted line with this sort of hip Eastern mysticism spouted by Maharishi and his kindred. But other New Agers offer palatable ramblings similar to Christianity, and here is the danger. *The movement undermines Christian beliefs through a deceptive overlap with Christianity.* For example, you can find these terms in New Age literature:

• God: This is usually an impersonal energy force, a cosmic consciousness. It could be male or female or genderless. It could be the earth, the sun or the moon.

• Christ: A reincarnated messiah, or messenger. This includes not only Jesus, but Buddha, Mohammed and others.

• Angels: Ascended masters. Upon close examination these beings usually more closely resemble demonic spirits.

• Born again: Reaching a higher dimension in life but not through salvation in Jesus Christ. It can boil down to letting a demonic presence take control of you. The most well-known born-again New Age experience is reincarnation. This amounts to a spiritual evolution, an upward progression by dead souls reappearing in new bodies. Furthermore, it amounts to a have-your-cake-and-eat-it-too deal: copping a spiritual experience without paying the price of repentance.

• Hell: New Agers believe in no specific hell as the Bible describes it. Hell for them can be an experiential thing; having a bad day might be seen as a day of bad karma (the force generated by a person's actions, as believed in Hinduism and Buddhism).

Whether it's through this kind of twisted terminology or an attraction to some other element, some Christians are being devoured by the New Age. For example, many read horoscopes, even though Scripture prohibits divination. Others fall into acceptance of bad karma—that they deserve their misfortunes because of sin and must endure them as something they somehow generated through their actions.

This brings up a key distinction between the New Age and Christianity. New Age does not preach that one should deny self and reach out to those who are suffering, as does Christianity. Seemingly, this would turn off those who expect a certain amount of compassion from any god and religion.

In a similar vein, the steep fees charged by some New Age practitioners limit certain elements of New Age to the well-off. On one seminar tour, for example, Shirley MacLaine was drawing three hundred dollars a person (times about one thousand people per evening) for her out-of-body tales. Salvation—free for the asking to those genuinely repentant, according to Christianity—is restricted to those with fat wallets under this pay-as-you-go religion.

Nevertheless, many people, including Christians, are drawn in. Teachers Irving Hexham and Karla Poewe-Hexham, the authors of *Understanding Cults and New Religions*, told in a *Christianity Today* article of a student who was impressed with Ms. MacLaine. Through her book and two-part television series, Ms. MacLaine has become well-known for popularizing channeling—people serving as mediums for spirit guides. The student considered herself a Christian yet believed in reincarnation. Fortunately, the teachers were able to steer her toward some exposes of the New Age movement that changed her mind.

Afterward the student reflected: "It's so clever. You accept one belief and then another, and before you know it you no longer feel comfortable with Christian beliefs. No wonder so many people I know cease to be Christian altogether."

Rising to Action

How can we take action against something that's so hard to pin down? Foremost, we must know Scripture. We cannot challenge these counterfeits of Christian terminology and Christian principles without precise knowledge of the real thing. We cannot expose as full-blown religions those occult-based philosophies that pass for simple motivational or self-improvement courses unless we know the fullness of Christ's kingdom and how Satan would scheme to undermine it.

With that knowledge, we can be prepared to blow the whistle when an employer tries to introduce New Age techniques into the workplace. Steve Hiatt did, and it cost him his job.

Hiatt was a senior manager for Tacoma, Washington-based Walker Chevrolet in late 1983 when he suggested the firm look into a training program offered by Seattle's Pacific Institute. He and his wife, Carol, attended a workshop to train facilitators so that he could then train the sixty employees at Walker.

The techniques taught included questioning truth, exercising mind over matter, and visualizing things and then programming the subconscious with this new reality.

"They told us that they were the same techniques that Hitler and Jim Jones used, but [the trainers] were using them for the right reasons," he said.

The workshop showed its true colors at a presentation one particular evening, which the leaders had touted as being life-changing. A very religious mood was set, and the participants were told about life after death. Furthermore, the real reason behind the training was revealed: to save the world.

After inquiring more about the program, Hiatt decided to quit the workshop early, resolving not to teach fellow workers principles that violated his convictions. In turn, Hiatt's employer of nearly ten years decided to release him. His firing led to a series of appeals yet to be resolved.

"We have seen a lot of good things come out of this," Hiatt said. "In 1988 the EEOC, which is the Equal Employment Opportunity Commission, issued a set of guidelines on New Age training in the workplace that were better than we could have written."

Hiatt has been willing to dig in for the long haul and fight. Even if he never wins in court, his former employer, as well as countless others who've read about and seen his case through coverage in the *New York Times*, "20/20" and other major media, will be much more cautious in checking out training programs.

"I'm not asking for any money or anything," Hiatt said. His intention is "to hopefully bring people's awareness up and get some case law so that companies might think twice before they force their employees to go through this type of training."

Incidentally, Hiatt's willingness to sacrifice his job security worked to his advantage. He gives credit to God that the termination resulted in the forming of his own Pontiac-GMC truck dealership.

While it's paramount that Christians take the trouble to defend their rights, how much better it would be if the church took the *offensive* in matters such as this.

For instance, everyone sees corruption in the business world, such as in shady Wall Street deals. The church, like everyone else, is wringing its hands, saying, isn't this terrible? Meanwhile, the New Age aggressors are popping up, saying, here's a better way to train executives and manage your company. And I'm not talking about just one grocery store in Atlanta or a car dealer in Washington. RCA, Procter & Gamble, Pacific Bell and other major corporations have experimented with New Age-type training.

The church should be offering alternatives. For example, I've heard of a Christian teaching a business ethics course at Northern Arizona University. This is one way to answer the call to action.

New Age is also penetrating the classroom, and you can bet it doesn't come in waving a religious flag that would set off First Amendment alarms. In Buffalo, New York, an elementary school teacher let her students try to do picture talking with Abraham Lincoln, George Washington and John F. Kennedy. This was called visualization. Yet it is the same heinous sin—reaching the dead through spirits—that Saul committed with a medium at Endor (1 Sam. 28).

In another classroom situation students were told to chant a New Age theme, something like, "All hail the power of the mighty globe, the world universe inside of us." Other public schools have incorporated yoga and meditation through a health text and the dangerous fantasy game Dungeons and Dragons as a means to enhance creativity.

These illegal intrusions of New Age practices in schools are in no way comparable to the equal access to school facilities that Christians are still having to fight for. The New Agers do not represent groups of students acting on their own after school hours. No reasonable Christian group is asking for the right to similar teacher-led practices, which would amount to in-class prayer meetings.

The introduction of New Age into public schools represents direct violations of the First Amendment and gross unfairness to Christianity in light of court decisions in recent decades. Christians must respond to the call to action to resist these illegal religious intrusions. The government's EEOC has clearly prohibited employers from coercive training programs involving things such as yoga and meditation. The EEOC is a good source to turn to for an appeal of New Age practices in the workplace. Nevertheless, we cannot count on the government, the ACLU or anyone else to be looking out for our interests.

In every area where New Age has an opportunity to infiltrate our lives, we must stand firm. New Age, for instance, has gained a definite toehold in popular music. Some music stores have entire sections for New Age music. Like its philosophies, New Age's music is a diverse bag that cannot fit a particular description, though it is mostly instrumental. The most dangerous New Age music contains subliminal suggestions or sounds or patterns, such as ocean waves, that aim to effect some kind of inner change in the listener. Purchasing the music by certain artists devoted to spreading the New Age gospel can only help them realize that goal. Like Christian musicians, New Age musicians have the opportunity to proselytize the audience between songs at a concert.

The New Age may be spreading the oldest lie—"You can be like God"—but there is no limit to human gullibility. We've seen that even Christians can be trapped in the allure of New Age, a spiritualized secular humanism that has no place for Christianity.

Because our religious freedom threatens its very existence, New Age will push Christ and His followers into a corner if we let it. We must challenge these deceptive philosophies wherever they appear. With the same vigor that libertarians have exercised in chasing Christianity out of public forums, we must forbid the government to establish New Age tacitly as the official or unofficial religion of our schools or workplaces.

FOURTEEN

BREAKING SATAN'S CHAINS

TOMMY SULLIVAN JR., a trophy-winning wrestler, made average grades at his Catholic school in Sparta, New Jersey. He enjoyed a good family life with his father, mother and ten-year-old brother, Brian.

When he was introduced to satanism in his eighth-grade religion class, Tommy told classmates the subject was too bizarre, something he would never dabble in. An April 1989 *Redbook* magazine article on satanism reviewed how, in a matter of weeks, he changed his mind.

Tommy began reading library books about the devil and witchcraft. He would shut himself in his room to listen to heavy metal rock music, repeatedly playing a song about killing one's mother. He tried to persuade friends to worship the devil with him, but they resisted. His school journal entries began showing things such as devils holding severed heads and promises to do work for the devil. One statement read: "DIE MOTHER FATHER BROTHER. SATAN IS MY PRINCE."

Tommy told a friend of a dream in which Satan, wearing Tommy's face, asked him to kill his parents. Tommy said he wanted to obey.

Four days later Tommy slit his mother's throat, carved her cheeks, gouged her eyes, partially cut off her nose and right hand, and smashed her back. He lit a fire in the living room, apparently to try to kill his brother and father. Tommy's body was found in a neighbor's snow-covered backyard the next morning, his wrist and throat slashed by his own hand.

An Ancient Religion

Satanism makes for great headlines and gory movies. At first glance it poses little threat to our religious freedom in America. After all, it seems to pop up in some *other* town. There's probably no Satanic Church listed in your local yellow pages.

But do not underestimate satanism. It is spreading. It is captivating the bodies and souls of vulnerable children.

"I went to one school where the satanist club was bigger than the Campus Life club," said *Edge of Evil* author Jerry Johnston, who ministers to youths about satanism, drug abuse and suicide.

Satanism's extreme forms advocate violence and death. Because it embodies everything opposed to Christianity, complete with barbaric rituals, it threatens the religious values we take for granted.

We've seen how once Christianity left the public schools, secular humanism invaded. It has come in many forms— amoral sex education, textbooks with Christianity censored out and classes that seek to destroy traditional values. The same climate that allows these trends has allowed satanism to begin permeating our schools and the rest of our culture with relatively little opposition. Consequently, we must be on guard against the same unfairness that has accompanied other beliefs; satanists must not receive privileges, such as unusual access to public forums, that are routinely denied to Christians. When they do, we need to raise hell—raise it to a level where satanism is exposed for what it is: a religion, and an evil one at that.

One reason satanism has made inroads in recent years is that most people mistake it for a lark. They may frown on the vandalism and violence that it produces, but mentally they rank it next to Santa Claus. They couldn't be more deceived. (Chalk one up for Lucifer!)

For starters, we know that at least as far back as the time of Moses Pharaoh had court magicians obviously advanced in the occult arts. They were able to duplicate the staff-into-serpent trick, as well as some of the plagues.

Satanism as we know it today goes back at least to the Druid religions of ancient Europe before Christ. Druids were the priestly class of the Celts. They worshipped many gods, sacrificed animals and possibly even humans. They practiced divination, partly through studying the remains of sacrificed animals.

Our present-day Halloween has its roots in the Celtic festival of Samhain, the Celtic lord of death. Druid religion died out after the Celts became Christians in the 400s and 500s. However, it was revived around the 1600s when Celts became interested in their heritage, and it still survives in Great Britain and Ireland.

In the United States you can categorize satanists in four classes. One follows modern organized groups, most notably the Church of Satan. A second group draws upon ancient satanic writings and tries to adhere to the old customs.

The third class is people, especially teenagers, who try to create their own religion under the umbrella of satanism, perhaps drawing upon the *Satanic Bible*, by Anton LaVey. For example, satanist students filled lockers in a Virginia high school with ritualistically sliced up cats and dogs. The students obviously had some kind of material to guide them.

A fourth category is criminals who use satanism as a pretext for their activities, such as mutilations and killings of animals and people.

Here there are two types of practitioners. One is a person religiously committed to satanism. The person will carry out the bizarre rituals as a matter of faith, much the same way a Christian will perform a ritual or attend a service in the belief that his religion requires it.

For example, a New Jersey pediatrician was accused of molesting his daughter. There was strong indication that he was abusing his daughter physically and sexually and that it was motivated by satanism. His putting hot water or hot wax into her genital area, it is believed, would not so much cause him to think of his child's pain but of giving glory to Satan.

The second category of satanist criminals would be the psychopaths who see satanism as an excuse to allow them to do things they've always wanted to do.

Satanism, in other words, is penetrating society in devious ways. Where the life and values of God are absent, Satan's temptations, his lies and his followers fill up the cracks. Every defeat dealt to the religious freedom of the kingdom of light is an advance for the kingdom of darkness. The church has done little to combat the growth of satanism, but there are ways to answer this call to action.

Spiritual Vacuum

What do satanists believe? Make a reverse image of Christianity and you will find out. Christians pray to Jesus; satanists pray to Satan. Light is a frequent theme of the New Testament, while satanists dwell on darkness and the color black. Christianity exalts life—supernatural, eternal life and physical life made in God's image; satanism thrives on death—mutilations, sacrifices, suicide pacts. Young people born again in Christ are joyful, outgoing, loving; teens drawn into satanism are withdrawn, sullen, typically focusing on drugs, death and the dark side of life.

Most tellingly, the Bible teaches that in *denying self* we find life and fulfillment; satanism says that fulfillment comes only through *exaltation of self.* Satanism pushes our greed button. Its adherents view all the rituals as means not only to glorify Satan but to glorify themselves, gain power and respect, to gain whatever they lack.

This, of course, coincides with what Scripture tells us of the devil's agenda. Just as he tempted Eve, he wants us to do things his way, not God's way. Satan's goal is death and destruction—of individuals, families, communities and, if God would allow it, all of creation.

We've seen how the expulsion of Christianity from our schools and our legal system has opened the door for secular humanism to enter as the dominant moral code. Satanism has flourished in much the same way. Like secular humanism, satanism tells its followers they can make up the rules as they go. They can be their own gods. And both philosophies say that everything that smacks of the Judeo-Christian heritage is obsolete.

Look at what has happened in school libraries. Court challenges have made it difficult not only to use the Bible in class but to keep it in some school libraries. Yet I never

171

hear of legal problems with the Satanic Bible, which is found in some school libraries. So you end up with a system that in some cases excludes the lawbook of the faith of our founding fathers yet permits a lawbook of the faith most explicitly hostile to Christianity.

There is seemingly no limit to where satanism will seep in as Christianity retreats from the front lines. It has appeared even in the U.S. military. A man in the U.S. Navy died in 1967. Having been a member of the Church of Satan, he had requested a satanic service at his burial in Arlington, Virginia. The matter went to court, and the court decided it could not deny him the satanic service because of constitutional protection of religion.

Another military case involves Lt. Col. Michael A. Aquino of the U.S. Army Reserve, founder of the Temple of Set, a satanic church in San Francisco. Aquino has a Ph.D. in political science and has been involved in psychological operations and other areas for the military. His writings have said only the members of his temple—numbering probably fewer than one hundred in 1987—would survive the apocalypse that he prophesied. He has referred to himself as the "Second Beast of Revelation." He acknowledges an interest in the occult rituals of the Nazis. The Army has known about his peculiar beliefs since 1981, yet he has since been promoted from major and received a top-secret clearance.

The Army has said Aquino has a right to his religious beliefs as long as they involve no illegality. This is probably for the best; that same freedom allows Christians to serve in the military. But Christians in the military, as elsewhere, must insist on the same freedom to express their beliefs that the satanists enjoy without someone attempting to gag them on the basis of church/state separation. It's hard to imagine that a Christian televangelist could rise as far in the military, or in any government position, as has Aquino, who publicly professes his prophetic role in a religion as bizarre and evil as satanism.

Heads in the Sand

As much as any other challenge to the lordship of Christ, satanism presents a call to action to the church. Sadly, Christians have not done much to combat satanism or minister to the needs of those trying to break the satanic chains that have bound them.

It's easy to get caught up in a placid Christian life-style of prayer, worship, fellowship and church activities. It's just as easy to ignore satanism, with its violence, its strange rituals, its unseen powers, its general unfamiliarity with Christians. To do so, though, is to dodge the Bible's commands to expose the deeds of the enemy, to shine God's light into the darkness.

Whether we are fighting in the prayer closet, the classroom or the courtroom, we know that "our struggle is not against flesh and blood, but against the rulers, against the powers, against the world forces of this darkness, against the spiritual forces of wickedness in the heavenly places" (Eph. 6:12). Paul goes on to advise putting on God's full spiritual armor: the breastplate of righteousness, the shield of faith, the helmet of salvation, the sword of the Spirit, loins girded with truth and feet shod with the gospel.

No general sends troops to battle unless they know what the enemy looks like, how he operates, what his strengths and weaknesses are. The church, likewise, must educate its members about their enemy, Satan. Paul, in 2 Corinthians 2:11, hopes that "no advantage be taken of us by Satan; for we are not ignorant of his schemes." This means knowing what Scripture says about this schemer. Every one of Christ's soldiers needs to be familiar with Satan's appearance in Genesis 3 as well as revealing passages in Ezekiel 28 and Isaiah 14.

We also need to learn to recognize signs of Satan's influence with our young people who are subject to satanism's lure. Anyone, of course, can be drawn into this web, but children from dysfunctional families are particularly vulnerable. Those with close family ties usually are resistant.

Those who've studied satanism and youth have found a pattern. School grades begin to drop. There is active involvement with things such as drugs, alcohol or animal rituals involving torture and mutilation. Moods change to surliness and anger.

Teens interested in satanism typically will narrow their circle of friends to only those who share one interest, such as heavy metal rock music, the occult or the game Dungeons and Dragons. This game, which calls participants to act out fantasies, has led to violence as serious as murder.

They may lock themselves in their rooms and play heavy metal groups such as Ozzy Osbourne, Motley Crue and Metallica. Lyrics by such bands sometimes endorse various forms of sexual activity and suicide.

Other signs are that notebooks may show drawings of 666 (the biblical symbol for the beast of Revelation), upside-down crosses or pentagrams (five-pointed stars, a satanic symbol). There may be a fascination with black. Girls, for example, may start wearing black makeup or nail polish.

Even children as young as three years old may show signs of satanic influence, though it may be nothing they have sought. Some modern Saturday morning cartoons, for example, introduce children to an unchristian world of the supernatural through tales of fantasy, mythology and superhuman power. Young children may show signs such as chanting, a premature interest in sexual activity or immense fears of the house burning up.

God can deliver young people who become ensnared in this web of self-destruction and death. Unfortunately, the church does not always want to take up where God left off. Too many Christians think ex-satanists are too dangerous to touch. Or they exaggerate Satan's power and fear what could happen by associating with one of his former disciples.

An evangelist friend of mine, John Jacobs, spoke with a former satanist when I was on a television call-in. The young woman was the daughter of a satanic high priest in Colorado and had been abused as a child. She called because she knew there was a way out and accepted Christ as her Savior.

When Jacobs asked if she had a message for Christians, she said Christians should not be afraid of people like her. Also, she said Christians profess their God to be stronger than Satan but don't always act like it. How could she believe if Christians themselves did not?

Christians have nothing to fear from Satan. Satan may have _power_ on occasion, but he has no _authority_. God the Father put all things in subjection to Christ (Eph. 1:22). The hexes and spells that satanists cast, hoping to wreak sickness, even death, cannot touch those who pray and act with the authority they have inherited through Jesus.

God's light outshines darkness. We have an obligation to keep the gospel shining in the forefront of every area of life. Young people exposed to the gospel in a regular, clear fashion will be much less susceptible to the wiles of Satan. That means proclaiming it in our families, our churches, our schools and our streets. The tragic fate that befalls teens like Tommy Sullivan is not the inevitable outcome of a sudden bite from a vampire bat that swooped out of nowhere. Parents who answer the call to action within their own families, and

Christian teens who work to extend the unconditional love of God to their friends, can defeat the enemy before he gains a stronghold in a young person's life. Satan may get away with some terrifying things, but we can beat him.

TAKING ACTION

THE OPPOSITION WAS formidable: the governor, the senate president, the speaker of the house, the labor unions and the Oklahoma Educational Association. All endorsed the proposed Equal Rights Amendment to the U.S. Constitution.

Oklahoma state senator John Young had a different perspective.

Young and some other senators shared concerns of many evangelicals, who have opposed the ERA on various grounds. These include the well-grounded fear that it could be used to further homosexual rights in every arena, or that it could be used to advance the cause of abortion.

Young's group began praying against the ERA's passage in Oklahoma. In spite of its strong base of support and the perception in that state that it eventually would pass nationally,

177

it was defeated.

Young credits the power of prayer. I couldn't agree with him more. Before discussing other avenues of answering the call to action, we must consider the main boulevard.

Secret Agent

While secular humanists see schools as change agents, there is another change agent, an invisible one, that packs a lot more horsepower. That is prayer. I would never want this book or the message of calling Christians to action to be viewed as separate from prayer. Christians could file lawsuits until the courts were backed up for years; they could hand out tracts on every street corner in America; but if these works were not accompanied by faith and by prayer, they would be dead. God is not under contract to bless every single thing done in His name.

The *real* spiritual warfare is not taking place in the court-room or in front of abortion clinics. It does not show up on videotape for the evening news. Rather, we are fighting "against the spiritual forces of wickedness in the heavenly places" (Eph. 6:12). You may be able to point to the con-venience store manager who refuses to remove pornographic magazines, or the school board member who stops at nothing to aggravate Christians, but the real sparks are flying in the spiritual realm. We can affect those battles with prayer. "The effective prayer of a righteous man can accomplish much" (James 5:16).

Prayer—or the lack of it—is in fact a major reason why this book is being written. Ben Kinchlow, formerly of the Christian Broadcasting Network, pointed out recently that the very fact that ministries such as C.A.S.E. are having to go to court to fight for the right of students to pray on school property says something very shameful: *America was not utilizing prayer enough to truly miss it when the Supreme Court removed it from schools.* Had prayer been an integral part of our private and public lives, its removal would have led to such a deafening roar that Congress would have taken some recourse—a constitutional amendment, perhaps—to remedy the heavyhanded court ruling.

If you don't use it, you lose it. We lost prayer and subsequently a lot more in the realm of religious freedom. That leaves us fighting to regain lost ground. It may be two steps forward and one step back, but at least we're winning. Christians across the nation, through prayer and involvement, are chipping away at the glacier that has advanced almost imperceptibly and crushed our freedoms.

As we survey our losses, it's easy to heap mounds of blame upon a liberal Supreme Court, close-minded school boards or a city council eager to restrict free speech. Yet we have to face the truth that governmental bodies basically represent the will of the people, whether it be the will of a true majority or a vocal minority. Therefore, we cannot expect that by reforming government we automatically will achieve a final solution to the problems of pornography, crime and abortion.

It's proper to work for civil laws that agree with God's law. It's foolishness, though, to think that right laws will change wrong hearts.

Second Chronicles 7:14 has long been a rallying cry for American Christians: "[If] My people who are called by My name humble themselves and pray, and seek My face and turn from their wicked ways, then I will hear from heaven, will forgive their sin, and will heal their land." Revival will originate with repentance and humility, not with the reversal of *Roe v. Wade.* Petitioning for revival should be an ongoing prayer burden.

At the same time, we need to be praying for those in a position of decision-making. This means the good guys *and* the bad guys. We are commanded in 1 Timothy 2:2 to pray for rulers and others in authority.

Furthermore, *prayer gives us insight to God's perspective on how to wage His battles*. Second Chronicles 20 tells how Jehoshaphat practiced the recipe to humble oneself, pray and seek God. Faced with attack by the Moabites, the Ammonites and the Meunites, Jehoshaphat sought the Lord and proclaimed a fast throughout Judah.

In the assembly he declared truths about God's omnipotence. As he continued in prayer, he reminded God of how He had cared for His people and had given them a land for a possession. He concluded: "O our God, wilt Thou not judge them? For we are powerless before this great multitude who are coming against us; nor do we know what to do, but our eyes are on Thee" (20:12).

God answered through Jahaziel, who told the people not to fear, "for the battle is not yours but God's" (20:15). God meant this literally. The people would not even have to dodge arrows on this one. The marauders turned on each other, littering the field with corpses (20:22-23). The Hebrews took three days to gather the spoil because it was so abundant.

Winning without physical combat was not the norm for the Hebrews, though it most certainly was God's way in this instance. Jehoshaphat and his officers would never have ascertained God's strategy without prayer. We, too, have that same obligation. God may have us do nothing but continue in prayer in a given situation. He may have us tangle with a city council for years over an issue of religious freedom. He may have us march around the walls seven times and shout. But unless His people humble themselves and pray, they will never find the Master's agenda for victory.

Hometown Goliaths

Most Christians underestimate the impact they can have on politics. It begins on the local level with actions as simple as signing petitions and registering to vote.

The San Francisco Board of Supervisors approved a "domestic partners" law in spring 1989 that would have bestowed legal status on homosexual couples. The mayor signed it in June. But opposing petitions with twenty-seven thousand signatures were presented one day before the law was to take effect, which put the measure before the voters in November.

Under this law, for a $35 fee homosexual couples and unmarried heterosexual couples could register their relationship with the city. This would guarantee the same hospital visitation rights that regular couples have. Homosexual city employees could have received bereavement leave, which would be no rare occurrence considering the incidence of AIDS in a city known as the nation's homosexual capital. A task force was looking into whether registered partners of city employees should receive health benefits. In other words, the city was moving toward having all its taxpayers fund various benefits for live-in boyfriends and girlfriends, homosexual and otherwise.

Most of San Francisco's elected leadership, as well as three dozen religious leaders from various faiths, backed the measure, according to an article in *World* magazine.

"We were David versus Goliath," said Jack Bellingham, speaking for the opposition. David's stone carried just enough velocity to fell this giant. The measure was defeated, 50.5 percent to 49.5 percent. With nearly 167,000 ballots cast, the deciding margin was only 2,000 votes. The power structure and the prevailing local intelligentsia had pointed toward a victory for the gay movement, but God enjoys upsetting the wisdom of man. God can do it in your hometown or your state capital just as easily.

Voting is one freedom Christians enjoy without some hot and bothered libertarian screaming "separation of church and state!" Yet so many of us do not bother to exercise this right. Whether we fail to vote for president of the United States or for a local school board member, we do so at our own peril.

The voting process is but the simplest of many ways Christians can answer in a physical way the call to action, illustrating their faith by their works. In the preceding chapters I have stressed the need to test evangelization in every public arena—schools, streets, sidewalks, beaches, parks and stadiums. Defending the right to proclaim the gospel in public places continues to be the mission to which C.A.S.E. is pledged. However, as further supports to religious freedom, there are other ways you can impact the political process and the affairs of the private sector.

Senators and Sausage

The old joke says that laws and sausage have this in common: If you saw firsthand how either one was made, you would have nothing to do with them.

That may be so. It can be frightening to see a state legislature in action, with the grandstanding and the inattention. (And this doesn't get beneath the sausage's skin— campaign contributions, bribes, vote trading and the like.) An observer might well wonder how any product could emerge from this bizarre assembly line and bear any semblance to justice and wisdom.

Nevertheless, laws will be made. If the Christian consensus is not heard, another one will be. Do not be deceived: If anyone tells you that you cannot legislate morality, remember that legislation *is* morality. It's just a matter of whose entrails get packed into the sausage.

More Christians need to reject their fear of inexperience, of making a mistake, and get involved in the process. Monitor county commission meetings, city council meetings, school board meetings, public hearings. Monitor anything that affects anything you care about.

You may not live in your state capital, but you can communicate with state representatives and senators by phone or mail. Let them know your concerns. Let them know when you think they're acting against principles you know to be godly. And don't forget to let them know when they're supporting the right causes.

The same goes for your Washington delegation. Even if your representative and senators do not have home offices in your town, they are eager to hear from you by phone or letter. You can bet they will respond if they plan on staying in office, though you may have to press them to get an unambiguous stance on controversial issues.

Regular contact can also lead to developing relationships with their staffs, particularly with Washington-level politicians. If you are well prepared in approaching them, able to supply helpful, objective materials, it will help them in doing their jobs and will further your goals.

When you focus on a particular issue be willing to form limited coalitions with strange bedfellows. If you are trying to outlaw X-rated movie houses or topless bars in your hometown, feminists may be willing to line up with your position.

Whether in your state capital or in Washington, D.C., you need patience to ride with a bill all the way. A measure does not simply get introduced and voted in or out in one swoop. A typical path is to go to a subcommittee following its introduction, then to a full committee and finally to the floor of the House or Senate. Alternate versions of the same measure that pass in both houses need to be resolved in a compromise committee and then back for passage in each house. Legislation may get proposed for several years before it ever reaches a full vote of both houses of the legislature or Congress. Citizens can communicate with lawmakers at any step in the process.

The communication, as well as attendance at legislative sessions, makes a difference. A Supreme Court decision in 1975 indicated it might be possible for states to regulate abortions of immature minors and require parental consent. In California a parental consent proposal was repeatedly defeated in a Senate subcommittee, though Christians were lobbying hard for the measure. The bill finally made it to the Senate Judiciary Committee, only to be defeated.

Yet Christians did not give up. They continued to support the measure visibly, and eventually it made it through the Senate and into the General Assembly, where Willie Brown Jr., speaker of the assembly, killed it. The next time through, so great was the outcry of Christians that even Brown, with all his power, couldn't stop it. The bill became law in 1988.

Unfortunately, the bill was ruled unconstitutional under the California Right to Privacy for Minors Act and has been tied up in the courts. But for it to go as far as it has shows the impact on legislation when there is visible, patient support.

Further Involvement

Not only can you impact the legislative process from the outside, but with a little determination you can make things happen on the inside. You can become involved at the precinct level, being a precinct officer. You can join committees at the local level of your political party of choice.

There are also platform committees at the national, state

and local levels. No candidate is totally committed to support a party platform, but the platform is meaningful nonetheless. The values expressed—as well as those avoided—present a current image for that party. The platform's "planks," or policy statements, represent a consensus reflecting all levels of the party. The omission of an issue—for example, the absence of a school prayer statement in the Democratic Party platform of 1988—indicates substantial difference of opinion within the ranks.

The two major parties sometimes adopt clearly opposing policies on the same issue. For example, in 1988 the Democrats supported "the fundamental right of reproductive choice," a kinder, gentler way of saying abortion, while the Republicans endorsed the fundamental right to life for the unborn child.

This is not to imply that Christians cannot be found in the Democratic Party, for they are there, just as they sometimes run as independents. Nor is it to say that the Republican Party has a hotline to heaven. In both parties Christians should participate in the platform process in the hopes of integrating godly values into their party's identity.

For a real taste of the democratic process, volunteer to work in a campaign. All things being equal, a dedicated group of volunteers willing to give generously of their time for a few months can easily be the deciding factor in getting a candidate in office.

Taking this one step further, run for office yourself. A political novice will not likely want to seek office in Washington, but why not a seat on the school board? Or your town or city council?

Write letters to the editors of your local newspaper or magazines you read regularly. Comment on current issues. Take issue with editorials or biased news coverage. Such letters are well read and help determine the moral/political climate of a community.

Contribute financially to pro-moral organizations. There are dozens of such ministries and secular organizations working in state capitals and Washington to monitor certain areas. They need your support. In return, most of them, such as C.A.S.E., have newsletters that can keep you informed of developments that usually do not get covered by the major media.

Affecting History

As the 1980s closed, people would ask me, "Aren't you excited about the Berlin Wall coming down?" I told them no; it looked as if the wall was simply being moved across the ocean. That's how severe the barriers are that have been erected around religious freedom in this nation.

Some Christians expect a handful of lawyers and their persecuted clients to resolve those infringements on our freedom. It won't work. We need more manpower and prayer power.

Laws and the traditions of men that unfairly limit us from the most basic of New Testament commands—to spread the gospel—call *all* of us to action. We cannot get involved on every front, but each of us can enlist to fight in the spiritual warfare that currently rages.

Randall Terry sensed a deep call for involvement. While he was in prison during late 1989 for his Operation Rescue abortion clinic trespassing, Terry spoke by telephone to James Dobson for his "Focus on the Family" radio show. Terry explained his motivation to Dobson:

> If thirty years ago, when you were a young man,
> if someone stood in your church, from a pulpit, and

said, "Thirty years from now we'll have murdered twenty-six million children. Infanticide and euthanasia will be practiced. We'll have a cocaine crisis that's out of control. We'll have women and children being exploited in pornography. We'll have snuff flicks where they kill people on film and people actually buy it. And a revival of Satan worship and human sacrifice and child abduction." If someone had stood in a pulpit and said that, nobody would have believed it....And so I ask, if we have plummeted this far in thirty years, where are we going to be thirty years from now?

Terry said that when his daughters grow up he does not want them to be able to ask him why he didn't do something to change the course of this country when he had a chance.

We still have that chance. So does our opposition, and they're doing more than chanting New Age mantras and picking colors for their Maharishi Electric Cars. They've attacked, and they're threatening to attack more. That's why C.A.S.E. takes as its motto the attitude of Peter and John in Acts 4:29 (NIV): "Now, Lord, consider their threats and enable your servants to speak your word with great boldness."

That's about all I can do. It seems to be working, but there are countless opportunities for others to jump in, to speak and act with confidence. People who answer God's call to action can become those who determine the course of history. Let's work together to leave a legacy of restored religious freedom. We have the opportunity to create a more fertile climate for our children and grandchildren to carry out the Great Commission to spread the gospel throughout the earth.

HOLDING A BIBLE STUDY
IN YOUR SCHOOL

Your legal rights. The Supreme Court ruled on June 4, 1990, that students have the right to use school facilities for religious meetings as long as the school makes the space open to other clubs on campus which are not related to the curriculum. *Westside Community Schools v. Mergens,* 58 U.S.L.W. 4720 (U.S. June 5, 1990) (No. 88-1597)

Taking action. Student religious groups meeting off campus should consider beginning an on-campus meeting, which has greater potential to attract the unsaved. At schools where there is no Christian student group, students should form one. Approach the principal and ask for meeting space on the same basis as other groups.

Overcoming resistance. If school officials refuse permission for a Christian Bible club or prayer group, explain that the Supreme Court ruled, in an 8-1 decision, that the federal Equal Access Act does not violate the establishment clause of the First Amendment. Thus, now the Equal Access Act guarantees in every state the right to hold student religious meetings, such as Bible clubs and prayer groups, on campus. The meetings do not constitute an establishment of religion. They do not violate the First Amendment. Therefore, the school cannot forbid student religious clubs to meet if other clubs are allowed to meet on campus and the school receives federal funds. The court ruled that Bible clubs or prayer groups, when officially recognized, must have access to the student activities program, the school newspaper, bulletin boards, the public address system and the annual club fair.

Explain that you are not seeking school endorsement of your group. If you are still denied permission, appeal to the school board on the same grounds. If the school board turns you down, seek legal help.

The court also indicated that student evangelism does not violate the establishment clause.

Further help. C.A.S.E., P.O. Box 450349, Atlanta, GA 30345.

INCLUDING RELIGION IN CLASS DISCUSSIONS

Your legal rights. Religion can be discussed objectively in any public school classroom. In early cases ruling against state-sponsored school prayer and Bible reading, the U.S. Supreme Court indicated that religion is still part of education.

For example, in *Abington v. Schempp*, Associate Justice Tom Clark wrote for the court: "It certainly may be said that the Bible is worthy of study for its literary and historic qualities. Nothing we have said here indicates that such study of the Bible or of religion, when presented objectively as part of a secular program of education, may not be effected consistently with the First Amendment."

Taking action. Students should be alert for opportunities to inject religion into academic discussions where it should normally arise. Ask questions about the role of Christianity in history. In any sort of discussion on a moral issue, raise the biblical perspective.

Overcoming resistance. If a teacher excludes discussion of religion in subjects where it should be allowed, explain that schools can approach religion on an academic basis as long as it does not become devotional. The school may strive for student awareness of religions but should not press for student acceptance of any one religion.

If the teacher seems resistant, either because of legal fears or hostility to religion, talk to the principal. Explain the freedom schools have to present religion objectively.

Because this is still a gray area for legal challenges, further appeal would be difficult.

Further help. Write C.A.S.E. for the brochure "Religion in the Public School Curriculum: Questions and Answers." This pamphlet explains what is allowed and what isn't regarding religion in public education. Give it to your teachers and principals. Point out that it is not a piece of narrow-minded religious propaganda, but that it is an objective consensus endorsed by the major teachers' organizations and several religious umbrella groups.

Parents and teachers more interested in this area might be helped by the books *Students' Legal Rights*, by J.W. Brinkley, and *Religion in American History: What to Teach and How*, by Charles Haynes, published by the Association for Supervision in Curriculum Development. ASCD's address: 125 N. West St., Alexandria, VA 22314-2798. This kind of information could also benefit Christian teachers who want to do more to include religion in their classes.

POSSESSION OF CHRISTIAN
MATERIALS AT SCHOOL

Your legal rights. The Supreme Court, in *Mergens*, reinforced that students have the right to bring their Bibles and other Christian literature or materials onto school campuses. It is legal to wear T-shirts, buttons and the like with Christian messages on them.

Taking action. Students should take advantage of the public forum their school campus represents by carrying their Bibles and otherwise visibly expressing their faith.

Overcoming resistance. If you are denied the right to have Christian materials, appeal to the principal. Explain that the Supreme Court suggested that student possession of religious material on campus does not amount to the establishment of religion, as prohibited by the First Amendment. On the contrary, the First Amendment protects all free speech.

If that fails, appeal to the school board.

Further help. C.A.S.E., P.O. Box 450349, Atlanta, GA 30345.

PROTESTING OBJECTIONABLE
CLASSES OR TRAINING

Your legal rights. While parents may have little direct say-so about what gets put into public school curriculums, federal law has given parents clear rights to exempt their children from experimental or values-related classes that depart from academics.

The Hatch Amendment, also known as the Pupil Rights Amendment, guarantees these protections. It says parents have the right to inspect all instructional material, including that used in experimental or testing programs. Unless parental consent is given, no student shall be required to submit to any kind of test designed to reveal information concerning political affiliations, potentially embarrassing psychological problems, sexual behavior and attitudes, illegal and anti-social behavior, critical appraisals of family relationships, legally privileged relationships (such as minister, doctor) and income.

If your school introduces practices that appear related to the occult or New Age—visualizing conversations with dead historical figures, chanting a mantra-like slogan, practicing any form of meditation and so on—then the establishment clause of the First Amendment works on your side for a change. Your rights have been violated because the state is attempting to establish a form of religion.

Taking action. The most important action for you to take in these sorts of cases is to find out on the front end what's happening. Don't wait for your child to come home with horror stories halfway through the school year, with much of the damage already done. Any sex education course, anything that appears remotely experimental on your child's schedule, needs thorough investigation immediately. Check the materials. Meet the teacher. Question your children from day one. If necessary, personally monitor the class.

Furthermore, stay in constant touch with your children about the content and teaching methods of what appear to be routine classes. A teacher can insert an unorthodox bias—amoral, anti-Christian, anti-family, anti-American and the like—into any class in a potent way without your ever knowing it.

Sex education: If your school system is beginning to introduce a sex education course, get involved. Lobby the school board or its designated committee to consider a traditional sex curriculum, such as Sex Respect. Any proper sex education course should teach abstinence as the primary and normal method of birth control prior to marriage. You will have to fight the charge that such an approach is unrealistic among today's licentious teenagers. Don't give in to such defeatist logic.

If your school system already integrates liberal sex educators such as Planned Parenthood or homosexual advocates such as California's Project 10, you probably have grounds to object. Such programs usually cross over from objective teaching to advocating amorality. Appeal to your school board that the course undermines parental authority by implying to students that everyone their age is having sex or by teaching that homosexuality is normal or by telling students that they can easily and confidentially arrange abortions without their parents' knowledge. If necessary, object on First Amendment grounds. Show that the state is illegally establishing a religion by advocating amorality.

As a more immediate tactic, find out what days the outside sex program representatives will be speaking to classes. Get concerned parents to take turns sitting in on classroom discussions. Planned Parenthood has been known to tidy up its presentations when parents are present.

Overcoming resistance. You should try to resolve any such objectionable classroom practice locally. Appeal to the teacher, then the principal, then the school board.

If those appeals fail regarding a clear example of a school trying to implement a New Age practice, legal action could prove successful on a First Amendment basis.

If appeals fail regarding values clarification or any sort of classroom therapy, the Hatch Amendment provides for parents to appeal through the U.S. Department of Education. Remember, this law does not prohibit the course, but it does prohibit your child from being included without your permission.

Do not be intimidated by the objection that a certain course falls outside the law because it was not developed with federal funds. The burden of proof is on the school to prove that the course used absolutely no tax money in its development, and this is unlikely.

Complaints should state all details of the violation. They can be filed through Family Educational Rights and Privacy Act Office, U.S. Department of Education, 400 Maryland Ave. S.W., Washington, D.C. 20202.

Further help. Concerned Women for America, P.O. Box 6545, Washington, D.C. 20035-5453.

To fight homosexual advocacy presentations. Traditional Values Coalition, 100 South Anaheim Boulevard, Suite 350, Anaheim, CA 92805.

PROTESTING TEXTBOOKS OR REQUIRED READINGS

Your legal rights. There is no clear definition about when parents have the right to demand alternate texts or outside reading when they consider assigned books to contradict family values. But challenges on this basis have been won. As to textbooks, you have the right to lobby for or against certain books. This is one way to work against the censorship of Christianity from textbooks and classroom discussion.

Taking action. Most state departments of education have textbook committees. Find out what grades they are working with, when the committee meets and so on. Write letters or attend meetings to voice your opinions. If you are sufficiently interested, work to get appointed to the committee.

Overcoming resistance. If a teacher insists on using objectionable texts or outside readings, appeals through the principal and school board and perhaps the state school board are in order. After that, legal action is required.

Further help. Concerned Women for America, P.O. Box

65453, Washington, D.C. 20035-5453. Rutherford Institute, P.O. Box 7482, Charlottesville, VA 22906-7482. National Legal Foundation, P.O. Box 64845, Suite 306, Virginia Beach, VA 23464.

HOME SCHOOL LEGAL PROBLEMS

Your legal rights. You have the right to teach your children at home at every grade level. State laws differ considerably as to the level of state involvement concerning curriculum, testing and reporting to the state and other requirements.

Taking action. If you are considering a home school, contact the Home School Legal Defense Association (address below) to find out a contact with a state-level home schooling chapter. Familiarize yourself with state and local requirements. Investigate several home school curriculums before choosing one that fits your needs. Try to comply with legal requirements that are not too burdensome and do not violate your convictions concerning authority of the parents and the state.

Overcoming resistance. If a conflict cannot be resolved locally, appeal through the normal administrative channels.

Further help. Home School Legal Defense Association, P.O. Box 159, Highway 9 at Route 781, Paeonian Springs, VA 22129. Phone: 703-882-3838. Rutherford Institute, P.O. Box 7482, Charlottesville, VA 22906-7482.

PUBLIC EVANGELISM

Your legal rights. You have the right to witness and hand out tracts on public property as long as you are not clearly disturbing the peace, such as using a bullhorn at 3:00 A.M. or interfering with public employees as they do their jobs. The fact that some passersby do not want to be bothered by evangelists does not make evangelism illegal.

You have the right to hold a religious rally or march on public property, though city ordinances vary on what sort of permits and arrangements must be required.

Taking action. Witness to Christ in all public forums—the busier, the better. Sidewalks, parks, beaches, airports, around stadiums, college campuses and post offices are places where you can legally evangelize, including distribution of material. Students at elementary and high school levels also can evangelize on their campuses. Malls, being privately owned, usually prohibit the distribution of literature, but they cannot stop you from having conversations with shoppers.

Overcoming resistance. If you have explained to officers your basic rights and the harassment continues, do not bother with bureaucrats, such as the parks director or stadium manager. Go straight to court and file a complaint.

Further help. C.A.S.E., P.O. Box 450349, Atlanta, GA 30345.

The Caleb Campaign is a ministry that helps public school students to proclaim the gospel by disseminating the *Issues and Answers* newspaper, which has interviews with Christian athletes and other religiously oriented articles. A court has found its distribution at a public high school to be legal. The Caleb Campaign, Box 174, Cary, IL 60013.

To learn the most effective methods for street evangelism, the ministries of Scott Hinkle and Jerry Davis offer excellent training for churches. Scott Hinkle Outreach Ministries Inc., P.O. Box 380306, Duncanville, TX 75138. Jerry Davis StreetReach Ministries, 703 Rayburn, Conroe, TX 77302.

FIGHTING ABORTION

Your legal rights. You have the right to picket on public property in front of clinics and hospitals that perform abortions.

Taking action. In addition to legal picketing, you can evangelize the patrons of abortion clinics on their way in and out.

Abortion alternative centers, such as Sav-A-Life and Birthright, use volunteers as counselors and for other work. They need workers, money and prayer.

Those centers also make referrals of some clients to shelter homes, where they can complete their pregnancies without the interference of unsupportive boyfriends or family members. Shelter homes in some states are subject to inspection by a government social worker. Couples with teenage sons are recommended not to open their homes for this ministry.

Write letters to your state and national elected officials, as well as letters to the editors of your local newspaper and other publications that are appropriate. Attend protests and rallies in your state capital when the legislature is in session. Abortion will be in the public consciousness for a long time. Christians cannot relent in expressing the truth about this horror or the opposition will dominate the public agenda.

Further help. C.A.S.E., P.O. Box 450349, Atlanta, GA 30345. National Right to Life Committee, 419 Seventh St. N.W., Suite 500, Washington, D.C. 20004. Christian Action Council, 701 W. Broad St., Suite 405, Falls Church, VA 22046; phone: 703-237-2100. Free Speech Advocates, 6375 New Hope Road, New Hope, KY 40052.

FIGHTING PORNOGRAPHY

Your legal rights. Communities have the right to regulate pornography according to local standards. That means restricting what is sold, where it's sold and who is able to buy it, and even prohibiting it altogether.

Taking action. *Locally:* Find out who's carrying what. Target convenience stores selling adult magazines, video stores renting adult movies, gift stores selling risque novelties and cards, and any other merchant that is purveying filth. Ask them to stop handling the objectionable material. Get your friends to make the same request.

If that fails, organize a boycott through your church. Try to coordinate it with other churches.

If that fails, talk with your city attorney about existing restrictions in your city ordinance. If you lack a tough ordinance, talk to your city council members about drafting an amendment. If your city has hard-core adult stores that carry nothing but pornography, work toward a law that would outlaw such stores altogether. Other cities have done this successfully. For other stores you may have to settle for zoning them to certain areas or implementing rules about sales and rentals to minors.

Nationally: Boycotts have proved effective against convenience store chains that stock soft-core men's magazines and against companies that advertise through objectionable magazines or television shows. Don't simply refrain from patronizing these stores or manufacturers; write them. Let them know you cannot in good conscience spend your money with them unless they break ties with pornography.

This goes for network television too. Let the networks know, by letter or phone call, what shows offend you. The TV moguls may not give a hoot for your morals, but they need you and the thousands like you as viewers if they expect to keep ratings high enough to draw advertisers.

Further help. Children's Legal Defense Fund, 2845 East Camelback Road, Suite 740, Phoenix, AZ 85016.

As a national resource, the American Family Association (formerly the National Federation for Decency) has for years led the way in fighting pornography and anti-Christian bias in the media. The group encourages boycotts and sends out an informative newsletter. Address: American Family Association, P.O. Drawer 2440, Tupelo, MS 38803. Phone: 601-844-5036.

FIGHTING NEW AGE TRAINING IN THE WORKPLACE

Your legal rights. You have the right to be exempt from motivational or psychological job-related training that is in any way religious or moralistic, whether or not it identifies with New Age.

Taking action. Explain to your employer the religious nature of the training and how it conflicts with your personal convictions. Explain that the Equal Employment Opportunity Commission has issued comprehensive guidelines that prohibit this sort of training.

Overcoming resistance. If that fails, you can file a complaint with the federal Equal Employment Opportunity Commission.

Further assistance. Equal Employment Opportunity Commission, Washington, D.C. 20507.

Chapter 4

1. Paul Kurtz, Humanist Manifestos I and II (New York: Prometheus, 1973), p. 16.
2. Quoted by Kirby Anderson, "About Pluralism and Religion," *Dallas Morning News*, October 22, 1984.

Chapter 6

1. *Rivera v. East Otero School District (R-1)*, 721 F. Supp. 1189, 1198 (D. Colo. 1989). (The court held that the school's ban which gave "the government the power to suppress speech in advance, while imposing no time limits or other procedural obligation on school officials, would insure that speech is suppressed to the minimum extent possible, or that speech is suppressed for good and expressed reasons, rather than at the whim of school officials.")

Chapter 12

1. Transcript of hearing, Attorney General's Commission on Pornography. U.S. Department of Justice, September 1985.
2. W.L. Marshall, "The Use of Sexually Explicit Stimuli

by Rapists, Child Molesters and Nonoffenders." *Journal of Sex Research*, Vol. 25 (1988), pp. 267-288.

3. Pope Study, "New Weapon Against Obscenity," *Paducah (Mich.) Sun Democrat*, June 3, 1983.

4. Quoted in *The Rebirth of America*, Nancy Leigh DeMoss, ed. (A.S. DeMoss Foundation, 1986), p. 103.

5. Phil Phillips and Joan Hake Robie, *Horror and Violence* (Lancaster, Penn.: Starburst, 1988), p. 187.

6. Phillips and Robie, p. 187.

Books

David Barton, *America: To Pray or Not to Pray* (Aledo, Tex.: Wallbuilder Press, 1988).

David Barton, *The Myth of Separation* (Aledo, Tex.: Wallbuilder Press, 1989).

Peter J. Ferrara, *Religion and the Constitution: A Reinterpretation* (Washington, D.C.: Free Congress Research & Education Foundation, 1983).

David Jeremiah, "The Porno Plague" in *The Rebirth of America* (Philadelphia, Pa.: The Arthur S. DeMoss Foundation, 1986).

Richard Kelley, *The Andy Griffith Show* (Winston-Salem, N.C.: John F. Blair, Publisher, 1981).

Tim LaHaye, *The Battle for the Mind* (Old Tappan, N.J.: Fleming H. Revell Co., 1980).

Peter J. Marshall Jr. and David B. Manuel Jr., *The Light and the Glory* (Old Tappan, N.J.: Fleming H. Revell Co., 1977).

Francis A. Schaeffer, *A Christian Manifesto* (Westchester, Ill.: Crossway Books, a division of Good News Publishers, 1981).

Phyllis Schlafly, *Child Abuse in the Classroom* (Alton, Ill.: Pere Marquette Press, 1984).

William Stanmeyer, *Clear and Present Danger* (Ann Arbor, Mich.: Servant Publications, 1983), quoted in Jeremiah.

John W. Whitehead, *The Second American Revolution* (Elgin, Ill.: David C. Cook Publishing Co., 1982).

John W. Whitehead, *The Stealing of America* (Westchester, Ill.: Crossway Books, a division of Good News Publishers, 1983).

Articles

Jerry Adler, " 'The Second Beast of Revelation,' " *Newsweek*, November 16, 1987.

K.L. Billingsley, "Gone With the Wind: Ted Turner's Strange Career," *World*, September 9, 1989.

The Rhode Island Pendulum, August 21, 1986.

Christianity Today, "Newspaper Admits Error," January 15, 1990.

Robert L. Cord, "Understanding the First Amendment," *National Review*, January 22, 1982.

Esther Davidowitz, "Die mother father brother," *Redbook*, April 1989.

Robert Digitale, "San Franciscans Reject 'Domestic Partners' Bill," *World*, November 18, 1989.

John J. Dunphy, "A Religion for a New Age," *The Humanist*, January/February 1983, quoted in Whitehead, *The Stealing of America*.

Billy Graham, "An Example for Us to Follow," *Decision*, November 1989.

Michael Ford, "Raw Power," *New Wine*, November 1983.

Karen Haywood, "Bible Reading on School Bus Takes Girl to Court," *World*, October 28, 1989.

Irving Hexham and Karla Poewe-Hexham, "The Soul of the

New Age," *Christianity Today*, September 2, 1988.

Maria Miro Johnson, "Ruling allows couple to refuse visit by School Committee for evaluation," West Bay (Rhode Island) *Journal-Bulletin*, August 13, 1986.

Los Angeles Times, "Judge Asked to Void Pierce Rules on Flyers," November 29, 1988.

David Neff, "Prime-time Shoot-out," *Christianity Today*, October 6, 1989.

Bob Pool, "Pierce College to Ask Court to Stop Leaflet Campaign by Jews for Jesus," *Los Angeles Times*, November 24, 1988.

Brian D. Ray, "The Kitchen Classroom," *Christianity Today*, August 12, 1988.

Timothy L. Smith, "Why Johnny Doesn't Know About Mennonites," *Christianity Today*, February 5, 1990.

Ken Waters, "Confronting the Movement That Seeks to Change the World," *Charisma & Christian Life*, May 1989.

Richard Zoglin, "Putting a Brake on TV 'Sleaze,' " *Time*, March 20, 1989.

For more information on how you can become involved in the ministry of Christian Advocates Serving Evangelism, please write to C.A.S.E., P.O. Box 450349, Atlanta, Georgia 30345.